The Book of

1

The Book of Ogham

The Book of Ogham

by
Michael Kelly

The Book of Ogham

Cover Illustration:
Ogham-carved stone from the Isle of Man

The Book of Ogham

Table of Contents

The Book of Ogham

The Book of Ogham

The Book of Ogham

Abbreviations

AIT   Ancient Irish Tales
BCE   Before the Common Era (= BC)
CE   Common Era (= AD)
OE   Old English
O.Ir.   Old Irish

A Note on the Pronunciation of Foreign Words --
In the text, Old Irish words are often followed by a guide to their phonetic pronunciation. These are contained in square brackets.

Acknowledgement

I would like to express my thanks and appreciation to Edred, whose encouragement led me to explore and rediscover the spirituality of my ancestors, and who gave me the opportunity and the challenge to revise and expand this book for its new edition.

The Book of Ogham

Introduction

The publication of the first edition of the Book of Ogham by Edred in 1992 marked a significant step forward in the recovery of an authentic Celtic means of divination and spiritual practice. Prior to the publication of this book, most volumes which purported to concern themselves with Celtic mysteries did so by trying to decode the mythologies of the Celts with non-Celtic keys, by applying the symbolism of other peoples to the Celts in inappropriate ways. What resulted was a hotch potch of materials available to the modern reader which were either incomplete, derived from romantic fantasy, or entirely non-Celtic.

The first edition of the Book of Ogham sought to remedy this situation by presenting an authentically Celtic key for the decoding of the Celtic mysteries. The ogham system is of significant age and is wholly and purely Celtic in its origins. Unlike much of Celtic lore, sufficient evidence survives from a sufficiently early period to allow us to reconstruct the ogham with a high degree of accuracy. Edred drew upon his extensive knowledge of Indo-European lore and his years of study of the Celts - including the Old Irish and Middle Welsh languages - and undertook just such a reconstruction. And once the ogham system was reconstructed, it was possible to apply its keys to reconstruct other fragments of obscure Celtic lore which would otherwise have been impenetrable.

The first edition of this book was primarily a manual of

The Book of Ogham

divination by means of ogham, although it was made abundantly clear that the uses of the system extended far beyond this. Its primary purpose, however, was to provide seekers after genuine, authentic Celtic lore with the keys whereby they could find it. It strove to provide the modern reader with a wholly objective reconstruction of Celtic cosmology, psychology and philosophy within a coherent body of symbolic meaning, to stand against the more subjective and fantastic renderings which had been offered up over the years. The primary goal of this new edition remains the same, but it has become necessary to update the original in two main ways:

1. New information on the original names and meanings of the ogham fews has come to light, which affords a glimpse even further back in time to their roots. This allows us to refine the meanings of the oghams still closer to their authentic original forms. It becomes apparent that the tree symbolism of the oghams, whilst important, is not quite so fundamental to their meaning as was originally thought.
2. A new edition of the book allows a couple of additional chapters to be incorporated, to expand knowledge of ogham into more obviously magical fields. A chapter is therefore included which illustrates how the fili can use ogham not only to read the patterns of manifestation through divination, but also to actively alter those patterns through the practice of magic, using the oghams as foci for the will. In order to facilitate the well-rounded and evenly paced initiatory progress of the practitioner, a suggested schedule for study and practice in measured stages has been incorporated into the book.

It is my wish that this book should assist every seeker after the ways and the wisdom of their ancestors, and that the ancient mounds of the sídhe may open their doors in response to our call.

Finally, my thanks to Edred for entrusting this revision and expansion of his work to my hands, it has been illuminating.

Michael Kelly, Ramsey, Isle of Man, Lughnasadh, 1999 CE

10

The Book of Ogham

Chapter 1
Oghamic Knowledge

The Roots of Knowledge

Ogham is just one of the many ways the ancient Celts encoded their secret wisdom. But of those ways it is one of the few we can still gain access to today. We can do this because enough clues were left behind from the genuine and authentic lore of the past to allow us to reconstruct the system from within the body of actual Celtic thought.

The ogham system is deeply rooted in the Celtic world view. Just as the Germanic runes were never used by Celts, ogham was never used by any other people. As such, it represents a unique and particular expression of wisdom within a certain set of symbols and myths. One might try to use ogham-wisdom to unlock the secrets of Greek mythology, but it would certainly prove to be a highly frustrating, not to mention deceptive, exercise. In like manner, the Celtic mysteries need to be approached through their own native symbol set.

So, who are / were the Celts? The Celts were an identifiable ethnic (national) and linguistic group of people who differentiated themselves from their Indo-European cultural matrix as early as 2000 BCE. The various Indo-European groups began to migrate out of the region of the Caspian Sea as early as 4000 BCE, with various

The Book of Ogham

individual linguistic and national groups differentiating themselves out of that larger primeval group at various times after that. The original homeland of the Celts – that is where a group of pre-Celtic tribes came into being as true Celts – seems to have been central Europe (approximately present day Switzerland, Austria, southern Germany).

Although now we so much identify the British Isles as being originally Celtic, these lands were not actually "Celticised" (by invasions of Celts from the Continent) until as late as 700 to 500 BCE.

From some early time there was a linguistic, and perhaps cultural, split within the Celtic world. This is exemplified in the language by a dialect split between the so-called P-Celts and the Q-Celts. The P-Celts are the Brythonic peoples of Britain and the Gauls, and the Q-Celts are the Goidelic tribes of Ireland – who also later colonised present-day Scotland. Examples of the differences in the languages can be shown through a look at the basic words for "four" and "five" in the two language groups.

	Old Irish	Middle Welsh
four:	cethir [kyethir]	pedwar [ped-war]
five:	coic [koyg]	pump [pimp]

These linguistic differences must have signified and led to a number of cultural differences as well. This is one of the reasons why we concentrate on the Irish tradition in this book. Ireland is where the bulk of the oldest mythological material is from and it is where ogham was most strongly represented.

It might be noted for those who, for whatever reason, wish to resist the idea that the Celtic mythology and religion (as well as culture) is essentially based on Indo-European roots that the first element in the names Ire-land and Ira-n are the same linguistically, and both are related to the Arya-ns of India. Thus the great span of Indo-European culture, from the middle of Asia to the westernmost islands of Europe, can be seen in its full expanse from ancient times.

The Book of Ogham

The Ogham System

Ogham is not like other writing systems, sacred or profane, which you might have encountered. It is really an alphabetic code rather than a standard alphabet as such. It is a system of numerical codes or signs which stand for sounds or letters. The sound system, as recorded in the medieval manuscript tradition, is as follows:

B	L	F	S	N
H	D	T	C	Q
M	G	GG	Z	R
A	O	U	E	I

From this arrangement, it can be seen that there are four groups (O.Ir. aicme) of five letters each in the system. From this, codes making use of these letters or sounds in this arrangement can be made. For example, the formula 1:4 would mean: first group, fourth letter = S. In classic ogham epigraphy (inscriptions) the system shown in figure 1.1 is used.

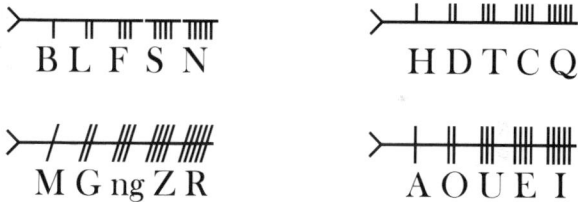

Figure 1.1: The Original Ogham System

At a later time there were five additional signs added to the ogham system to represent diphthongs. That these are later additions and not part of the original system is shown both by the Irish name for them (forfedha) which means "additional tree or letter", and by the fact that these signs are not used in the pre-medieval inscriptions. However, it

The Book of Ogham

is important to note that the forfedha are cosmographic signs of traditional value – but it is also important to see that their esoteric function is substantially different from those of the basic twenty oghamic fedha, or "fews" as they are called in Anglicised form.

Table 1.1: The Historical Forms of the Forfedha

Shape	Sound	Name	Meaning of Name
	ae	phagos	beech
	io	iphin	gooseberry
	ui	uileand	honeysuckle
	oi	oir	spindle
	ea	ebad	aspen (alternate name of E-few)

It should be noted that the names of the forfedha are not as essential as those of the other fews. They were certainly added at a later time. There is substantial disagreement among scholars as to the forms and names of these fews. But here we have symbolic shapes to guide us in our determination of their cosmological and divinatory meanings. The forfedha clearly stand outside the normal numerical sequence of the twenty fews of the basic system.

What is essential to realise about the secret of the oghamic tradition is that it is a numerical code based upon a set of sounds. This becomes quite clear when you see that the bardic system of classification of things is based on the fact that things belonging to one secret class or another all start with the same sound. This is understandable on one level because those things which have names that start with the same sound will alliterate in the bardic kind of poetic composition – and in this way will further reveal the hidden and poetic connections between the words.

The oghamic system consists of three components:

1. sound
2. name(s)
3. number(s) [order and binary indication of its place in the system]

14

The Book of Ogham

The sound and the name are linked by the acrophonic, or "first-sound" principle, while the numerical code both reveals the sound and conceals it behind a veil of esoteric knowledge. All of these aspects have an importance of their own.

The structure of the ogham system is determined by two factors: 1) shape (i.e. the kind of shape a sign has) – which determines the aicme of the sign, and 2) number (i.e. how many of these kinds of shapes there are) – which determines the position of the character inside the aicme.

Many variant forms of ogham based on these principles of construction are found in the text of The Book of Ballymote. These are based on a technique very similar to that used in the construction of runic codes among the Germanic peoples. For example, the distinct consonants of "shield ogham" (O.Ir. ogam airenach) appear:

Originally the names of the ogham characters designated various things, e.g. plants, concepts, metals. The majority of names were, however, plant names. At some time in the early Middle Ages the names underwent a reform by which all the letters were designated with plant-names. This reform had profound effects. In fact the Irish (Gaelic) word for "letter" -- as well as ogham character – remains the word fiod (O.Ir. fid), which primarily means "tree". But actually the ogham system was first and foremost, and from the very beginning, a system for the bardic and druidic classification of all things. Trees were of great symbolic importance in this tradition, and so the tree names of the ogham characters became the primary or standard ones.

as "irrational" as it might seem today, the ancient Celtic wise-folk saw a secret connection between words that began with the same sound. This link, in the heads of the words, is a strong esoteric connection that surfaces in the poetry of the bards. In many ways this is similar to the way the Hebrew Kabbalah makes secret linkages

15

The Book of Ogham

between words which add up to the same numerical values using the system of gematria. There may be no logical or obvious link between them but the correspondence in sound or number points to an otherwise hidden sympathy.

The Technical Vocabulary of Ogham

When talking about actual oghamic inscriptions or writing, there are certain technical terms which must be understood. The line along which the ogham characters are carved or written is called the "stemline" (O.Ir. flesc). Any piece of ogham writing is usually begun with a so-called "feather sign" ➤ which marks the head or beginning of the writing and indicates the direction in which it should be read. The marks creating the consonantal characters are referred to as "scores", while those forming the vowels are called "notches". Of course, as already mentioned, the characters themselves are actually called fedha (plural) or fid (singular), which literally means "wood" in Old Irish. "Few" is an Anglicised rendering of a later form of this word (fidhu or fiuth). So you may hear the characters of the ogham system commonly referred to as "fews".

The Origins of Ogham

How the ogham system came into being is a topic of great interest to those who would unravel the secrets of that system. Scholars have not been in agreement about this in the past. Seemingly there are two different problems when trying to solve the riddle of ogham origins. Ogham appears on one level to be a number-code more than an "alphabet", yet its structure is decidedly alphabetic. So one set of problems belongs to its particular number-code system and another belongs to the question of what (if any) alphabetic system was used as a model underlying that code.

It appears, from the general distribution of ogham

The Book of Ogham

inscriptions, that the place of origin was far southern Ireland, with the highest density in the modern counties of Kerry, Cork and Waterford. This is also the area of the island which was first missionised by the Christians – before Patrick, who was active in the north. It is also an area which had maintained close cultural ties with the continent of Europe. Evidence seems to point to a monastic cultural milieu for the matrix in which the ogham writing system was invented.

There are two different problems when trying to determine the origins of ogham. This is because although the ogham system is based on an alphabetic one, it also makes use of a numerical encoding system called the "signary". The signary is a system whereby a sound can be signified by a combination of two numeric indicators: e.g. 1/2 (= group 1, sign 2). This example would be a way of signifying L in the ogham sequence, which is the second character of the first aicme. The second question revolves around the source alphabet or phonetic system underlying ogham.

The cultural matrix for the creation of the ogham system was probably the increasingly Christianised southern and south-western rim of Ireland in the 3rd or 4th century. The oldest know ogham inscriptions date from the late 4th century – but as a rule the origin of a writing system can be presumed to predate the oldest attestation by one to two hundred years. This is because the earliest uses were probably sparse and on highly perishable items.

The original ogham system seems to have been created for the sounds of Primitive Irish, the historical stage of the language which just predates Old Irish. This is why there are the apparently redundant letters quert/cert and nGétal, which stood for /kw-/ and /gw-/ respectively. These sounds disappeared in Old Irish, and fell together with /c/ and /g/. However, the system was already traditionally set, and so every effort was made to preserve it intact by reassigning values to the unneeded characters.

Clearly ogham was a system set up in some sort of contrast, if not competition, with the Latin / Roman letters. The numeric encoding of the system is most plausibly explained by the desire for secrecy as this is a subject never far from references to ogham.

17

The Book of Ogham

The Signary

There are three major theories on the origins of the signary aspect of the ogham tradition: 1) the manual gesture theory; 2) the hahalruna theory, and 3) the tally-stick theory. The hand gesture theory was originated by R.A.S. Macalister who theorised that it was a silent sign-language invented by Gaulish druids around 500 BCE. This theory has fallen out of favour among scholars as it does not fit the known cultural evidence or chronology of ogham origins. A date of 500 BCE for the origin of ogham is simply too early.

The hahalruna theory stems from a medieval manuscript called the Isruna Tractate from the late 8th century (Derolez 1954, 120ff.) wherein encoded forms of the Germanic futhark are outlined in ways that very much resemble the theory underlying the ogham signary. The Germanic runes are divided into three groups of eight staves each and can be signified by any two-termed indicator: 1-3/1-8. For example, a line with two strokes to the left and three to the right would signify second group, third rune = isa. The earliest evidence that the futhark was divided into three groups of eight (called ættir in Old Norse) goes back to the Grumpan bracteate, which may date from as early as 450 CE. This theory was more widely supported some decades ago, but it has its own problems of chronology. The earliest possible attestation of this kind of runic cryptography is the ring of Körlin, which is perhaps as early as 550 CE. This is several hundred years after the origin of the ogham system. It may in fact be the case that the runic codes have the ogham as their inspiration rather than the other way around. (Derolez 1954, 153; 161.)

Among the scholars today the most widely held theory on the origin of the ogham signary hinges on its nature as a tally – as a numeric encoder. The kind of tally represented by ogham is derived from the most basic method of grouping every five numbers in some distinctive way, e.g. IIII = 4; V = 5 in the (old) Roman system. Tally sticks had been common since the Stone Age. All the ogham signary did was simply assign sound values to the numbers 1 – 20 – conveniently and naturally grouped by fives. The original formulaic limitation of the number of signs to 20 is intuitively correct in light of

The Book of Ogham

the importance of this unit reflected in the Celtic languages.

It seems most likely that an ancient tally-system was the underlying basis for the ogham signary. This theory raises no chronological problems, as the tally-system was ubiquitous, and it has no cultural objections, as it requires no positing of outside influences. It is the simple, autochthonous solution to the problem of the origin of the ogham signary.

The "Alphabet"

The alphabet or phonetic system used by the originator(s) of ogham poses a different problem from that of the signary. The signary could have been used to encode the phonetic system offered by the Greek alphabeta, the runic futhark, or the Roman ABC.

There are indications in the works of Classical historians and ethnographers that the continental Celts used the Greek alphabet for certain kinds of profane written communication. but that their secret lore was not committed to writing. Caesar says (in The Conquest of Gaul) that the druids believed their teachings would be profaned by being written down. This same attitude met the arrival of literacy in India at the time of Alexander – the Brahmins shunned it for the same reason. It was only later that writing was secularised for religious and magical purposes.

It is useful to know that the Celts were using the Greek script in the last few centuries BCE, because it is clear that the ogham is not an original system. A system such as that represented by ogham (essentially a code) must have an alphabetic structure well known to the encoder at work behind the scenes. The alphabetic system is the key to the numerical code represented by the ogham characters.

Macalister's theory was that the Chalcidic Greek alphabet underlies the ogham system. This was in use in northern Italy in the last few centuries BCE. This system was sometimes used to write Celtic and, so this theory goes, sometime between 200 BCE and 200 CE the oghamic system was created within druidic circles on the Continent and then exported to southern Ireland. This theory has

The Book of Ogham

few adherents among scholars today.

But what was the nature of the system originally? There are no ogham inscriptions on the Continent of Europe. So if the system originated there, it is unlikely that the inscribed system of scores as we most commonly know ogham today was in use. Macalister thought that the system was invented as a kind of sign language which the druids could use to communicate with one another secretly. This was speculated to be a form of code using the five fingers of the hand as the basis of the code – as we see in the so-called "foot ogham" (O.Ir. cossogam) from the Book of Ballymote. (Calder pp. 296-97)

In cossogam the bards use the fingers of their hands in various positions along their shinbones to indicate the oghamic code. The fingers will be put to the right of the shinbone for the B-aicme, to the left for the H-aicme, diagonally for the M-aicme, and straight across for the A-aicme. The number of fingers used will indicate which few of the group is meant. For example, two fingers placed to the right side of the shinbone would mean the L-few. It is just as likely, however, that these practices are late developments rather than clues to the origin of ogham.

Chiefly based on the ideas of the runologist Helmut Arntz a case can also be made for the older Germanic futhark as the sound-system underlying ogham. Among the best points in favour of this theory, besides similarities in purpose and character of the runic and ogham systems, are: 1) the special sign for the /ng/ sound (necessary in Germanic, but not in Irish), 2) the distinction between vocalic and consonantal /u ˜ w/, 3) the ease of derivation of ogham H and Z from the futhark, and 4) the lack of /p/ in ogham and the rarity of the p-rune in runic inscriptions.

There are no chronological problems with this theory as the runes may have their origin as early as 200 BCE, several hundred years before the probable date of the origin of ogham. But culturally there are significant problems with this theory. Arntz speculated that the ogham was invented by a Pict, a non-Celt familiar with both the Celtic and Germanic cultures. This would be, according to Arntz, the most plausible cultural bridge between Scandinavia (epicentre of the runic tradition) and southern Ireland (the place where ogham came

The Book of Ogham

into being).

In opposition to the Greek and runic theories is the idea that the Roman alphabet underlies the sound-system. This theory holds the high ground among scholars today. The essential reason to identify the Roman alphabet as the prototype for the ogham system lies in the cultural / historical field, as Latin and hence the Roman ABC would most likely have been familiar and readily available to the inventor of ogham (pagan or Christian) living in southern Ireland in the 4th century CE. Additionally, there are structural arguments in favour of the Roman ABC: 1) ogham sounds are grouped according to the Latin grammarians' classification of letters, i.e. vowels, semi-vowels and mutes. 2) A and B are the initial vowel and consonant in both systems respectively. 3) Both the Roman ABC and the ogham are restricted to five vowel sounds. 4) Both ogham and the Roman system distinguish between the /k/ and /kw-/ sounds.

Perhaps on structural grounds the runes have as much to recommend them as the Roman alphabet, but as McManus points out, the runes do not have enough in their favour to oust the Roman system from the position it enjoys by virtue of its cultural prevalence in the exact region of ogham origins. Also, as when considering the origin of the runes, we must reckon with a high degree of creativity and inventiveness on the part of the "first oghamist". Ogham's unique essence and its persistence in history are strong indicators of the vitality of the subculture which created and first nurtured it. Whatever its ultimate source, the ogham system was not a passive partner, but an active re-innovator of the system which inspired it. Its divisions, names and methods were unique and original in the annals of alphabetic history. It is perhaps on this uniqueness and independence that our thoughts should dwell most profoundly.

Mythic Origins of Ogham

One Irish source tells us that ogham was first invented by a heroic god named Ogma. The Irish In Lebor Ogaim, part of the Book of Ballymote, provides us with the following information:

21

The Book of Ogham

What are the place, time, person and cause of the invention of ogham? Not hard. Its place is Hibernia insula quam nos Scoti habitamus (The island of Hibernia, where we Scots - Irish - live). In the time of Bres, son of Elatha (Poetic Art) king of Ireland, it was invented. Its person Ogma, son of Elatha, son of Delbaeth, brother to Bres - for Bres, Ogma and Delbaeth are the three sons of Elatha, son of Delbaeth there. Now Ogma, a man well skilled in speech and poetry, invented the ogham. The cause of its invention was that he wanted to prove his ingenuity, and that he thought this language should belong to the learned to themselves - to the exclusion of farmers and herdsmen. Ogham got its name from Sound and Matter - who are the father and mother of ogham...

With respect to Sound, Ogham comes from Ogma, its inventor. But as far as Matter is concerned, ogham is ognaim -- "perfect alliteration", which the bards applied to poetry... For the poets measure Gaelic by letters (O.Ir. feda). The father of ogham is Ogma, the mother of ogham is the hand or knife of Ogma.

Unfortunately we do not have detailed myths about Ogma or how he invented the ogham system. In order to gain further insight into this god, we must go to Gaulish sources. The Greek historian Lucian (2nd century CE) reports about a fresco he saw in southern Gaul which depicted Hercules as an old bald man leading around a troop of men by means of a chain of gold and amber running from his tongue to their ears. All of the men are smiling and happy, as is their leader. Lucian was told by a learned Gaul that the Gauls knew Hercules as Ogmios, and that he was shown in this form in the fresco because eloquence was considered by the Gauls to be stronger than physical strength, and that it was in fact at its peak in old age.

But oddly enough there seems to be no sign of a cult of Ogmios on the Continent. His name only appears on two curse formulas inscribed on lead plates.

Besides the passage quoted from The Book of Ballymote, the only other substantial reference we have to Ogma in Irish

The Book of Ogham

literature is found in "The Second Battle of Mag Tured", where we read that Ogma, the champion of the Tuatha Dé Danann, "... found Orna, the sword of Tethra, a king of the Fomorians. Ogma unsheathed the sword and cleansed it. The sword then recounted everything that had been done by it – for it was the custom of swords at that time, when unsheathed, to pronounce the works that had been wrought by them." Here too there is a magical component of eloquence and perception.

The only other clues we have to myths concerning Ogma all revolve around the theme of men being led by chains attached to their leader. There is an ancient Amorican coin with this motif, and there is an obscure reference in the "Cattle-Raid of Cooley" to a man who has around his neck seven chains, to each of which are attached seven men whom he is dragging around.

It is most likely, despite some etymological problems, that the Irish god Ogma and the Gaulish god Ogmios are the same. What is unusual is that an apparent warrior would govern matters of speech, eloquence and magic. But as we have seen with the Germanic tradition, such shifts are by no means unknown. There the god of magic, Woden, takes on warrior characteristics.

The derivation of ogham writing from Ogma is apparently the more purely pagan version, which has no overt reference to biblical narrative, usually obligatory in medieval traditions. There is, however, also an alternate tradition which does take biblical mythology into account. But even it is only superficially "Christian". This alternative is found in the Auraicept and relates the tale of a certain Fénius Farsaid who was an important scholar learned in the three great languages of the Judeo-Christian tradition: Latin, Greek and Hebrew. It is said that he set out on an expedition from Scythia along with two other important scholars: Goídel mac Etheoir and Iar mac Nema and a retinue of 72 additional scholars. These 75 learned men made their way to the "Plain of Shinar" -- where the Tower of Babel stood. (Cf. Genesis) Under the direction of Fénius Farsaid, who stayed behind in the tower to direct their studies and to provide for their sustenance, the other scholars went out among the confused languages of the world and for ten years they studied them and reported back to Fénius. Their master then created a language from the collected data, a language which only the scholars would know. This was called the bérla tóbaide, or "selected language" which was named Goidelc after one of the scholars. Besides this language, two others were invented and the ogham writing system as well, as a way to write them. The 25 most notable scholars from the retinue lent their names to the letters of the ogham system.

Although this story is an obvious attempt to place the origin of the ogham system in the context of Judeo-Christian mythology, it remains a rather pagan, or paganising, account. First, the whole rationale of the story seems to be to reverse the will of God, who had confused the languages of the world in the first place. Second, this is a rather sophisticated account of how scholars coordinated their efforts to create the system artificially and rationally. as such it reflects something of the essence of what must have actually happened not literally but rather figuratively on the "Plain of Shinar". This would explain why the ogham system is so rationally ordered, with vowels separate from consonants, and so on. Nevertheless, this second myth explaining the origin of the ogham system would seem to have been a more "Christian" alternative to the story of the pagan god Ogma as its inventor.

The Uses of Ogham

The ogham system is first and foremost a system of classification of things in a cosmological order – which in turn acts as a powerful aid in the process of memorisation. It must be borne in mind that the ancient druids did not write their lore down, but rather had to commit it all to memory. The curriculum of training as a druid may have taken as long as twenty years. Tools for the strengthening of memory were, therefore, essential to druidic training. The intelligible ordering of things in the worlds and the ordering of words which signified these things is, on a real level, tantamount to a kind of cosmology. So the ogham system, far from being an arbitrary set of conventional signs (such as our alphabet now represents) is a complete cosmic index or guide to how things are organised in the multiverse.

In poetry, the usefulness of the system is obvious – it relates the world of sound to the world of meaning in a direct way. But the druids were more than "just" poets. That is, "poetry" is actually a part of something much greater – which we might be tempted to call "science" today. Ogham is a system for the organisation of all disciplines of thought – be they the natural sciences, magic, religion, poetry, art, medicine, or law. In these disciplines ogham enables the practitioner to classify and memorise that which he or she needs to know and have embedded deep within the soul.

How this relates to magic and divination as such should be obvious. If magic is an art and/or science of creating change in the cosmos through exercise of the will, then the mapping and classification of that cosmos is essential to the aims of magic. Ogham is a traditionally scientific map of the cosmos. By the same token, if divination or oracular activity is the art and/or science of obtaining meaningful messages from the cosmos or spiritual structures within it, then that same cosmic map remains essential to being able not only to receive the messages but also to being able to decode them.

Besides the evidence we find in the Book of Ballymote and other Irish manuscripts of the Middle Ages, the other main body of evidence we have for the ogham tradition comes from ogham inscriptions themselves. The majority of these are "memorial stones" carved to memorialise a dead man and/or to call on the gods or semi-divine ancestors of the man to help him in the Underworld. These inscriptions are not very long and they are extremely formulaic.

Ogham Inscriptions

Actual inscriptions in ogham characters are only found on the British Isles. In all there are some 350 known ogham inscriptions, mostly carved in what is known as the Ogham Age from about 300 to 700 CE. There appear to be only a few genuine ogham carvings later than this, although knowledge of the system passed on orally for generations before it was recorded in medieval manuscripts such as

The Book of Ogham

the Book of Ballymote. There are some inscriptions made in the medieval period which obviously draw on the kind of knowledge preserved in the scholastic manuscripts.

Of the known ogham inscriptions 300 are found in Ireland (mostly in the extreme south) and the rest are on the Isle of Man and in Wales and Scotland. Most of the stones are in Irish, of course. However, a few of the Scottish stones are perhaps Pictish - or non-Celtic - and can not be decoded.

Most typically an oghamic monument is a standing stone or monolith with squared or sharp edges on which the ogham is carved. These stones may have been used to mark sacred sites, but more usually they were markers of the frontiers or borders of a tribal territory or property lines.

Technically, the sharp edge of the stone would act as the stemline for the ogham, and most typically the ogham would be written from the bottom toward the top of the stone. If it continued, it would start to come down the adjacent edge of the stone. Rarely the ogham characters would be carved onto the flat face of a stone (with or without an established stemline).

The contents of the inscriptions fall into two categories:

> I.   Memorial / invocatory (on stones)
> II.   Magical (on loose objects)

The second category is not very well represented, with only a handful of examples. The first kind of inscription, however, has several subtypes. All of these could be considered "memorials", but they often seem to be calling on the dead man, his ancestors (or his gods who may be his ancestors) at the same time. In these formulas, the form N.N. stands for a proper or personal name.

A.   N.N.'s (stone) = This type just has the possessive form of a personal name. They are probably memorials to the dead.

B.   ANM + N.N. = ANM (O.Ir. ainm) means "name" - so this kind of inscription essentially says: "In the name of N.N.!" These are either memorials or property markers.

C. N.N. MAQI N.N. = "N.N. son of N.N." Sometimes the ANM is also prefixed. These are memorials as well.

D. N.N. AVI N.N. = "N.N. grandson (or simply descendant) of N.N." This names an ancestor more remote than the father.

E. N.N. NETA N.N. = "N.N. nephew of N.N." Here the uncle of the memorialised man is named.

F. N.N. CELI N.N. = "N.N. follower, client or devotee of N.N." Here the second name may be that of a god or a remote semi-divine ancestor.

G. N.N. MAQI MUCCOI N.N. = "N.N. son of the descendant of N.N." Here again the last name is often that of a god.

H. N.N. MAQI N.N. MAQI MUCCOI N.N. = "N.N. son of N.N. son of the descendant of N.N." Which is an elaborate version of type G.

I. N.N. KOI MAQI MUCCOI N.N. = "N.N. the son of the descendant of N.N." Here the dead man is identified as the pre-eminent or chief descendant of a divine or semi-divine ancestor.

Time has not been kind to the ogham inscriptions. Because they were carved on the part of a stone most likely to suffer from the elements, they are very often so badly worn away that interpretation is difficult or impossible. But the elements were not the main enemy of the inscriptions.

Ogham may have come into use in the form of inscriptions in late pagan times – or in a time of "mixed faith" -- but the system as a whole, and even the inscriptions themselves, appear to reflect the pagan, pre-Christian Celtic culture. As such they appear to have been targeted for destruction by clerical thugs or devout converts to the foreign religion. There are clear traces of efforts to scrape away the ogham on many stones. In the case of those stones which probably bore the name of a Celtic god or goddess (for example the last name on stones of types F-K) special care was taken to obliterate the name totally. Some scholars have theorised that the newly Christianised clan did this to try to cover their pagan past. The reasons remain obscure, but the fact that the stones were defaced for religious purposes seems clear. It may have been that at certain times and places the very use of ogham itself was suspect as pagan activity, while at other times it was merely the pagan importance of divine ancestors that the clerics opposed.

Besides defacing the stones, it is also thought that Christians would try to "sanctify" or "exorcise" the stones by carving Christian crosses on them.

Actual ogham inscriptions often have irregularities of spelling and artificially archaic forms of language. These irregularities may have been intentional and have had some esoteric importance. But it must also be kept in mind that perhaps the man who actually knew ogham was not the man who in fact did the carving. It may have been that one man "a scholar" (fili) executed the ogham on a stick or on a wax tablet, and a stone mason, who was completely ignorant of ogham, was the one who actually went out into the field and carved the stone. This pattern of activity is also sometimes found in the runic culture of the Germanic peoples.

There are indeed a number of pseudo-oghamic inscriptions (also called "plough ogham"). These are not true ogham at all, but rather superficial imitations of the script. It is thought that these represent frauds perpetrated on unsuspecting folk who paid unscrupulous oghamic con-men for memorials to their dead ancestors. It is certain that the carving of true ogham memorials was a professional activity of the old druids – otherwise the con-men would not have been able to move in during the Christian period.

The only comprehensive edition of the ogham inscriptions is that of Macalister. From his collection, we can draw a few examples to show what actual ogham inscriptions are like. Although there are not many overtly magical inscriptions, two examples can be found which are probably "words of power" inscribed onto magical objects. One is the sheep-bone from Tullycommon (County Clare, Ireland). The ogham writing on it appears:

The Book of Ogham

This can best be transcribed: IACS, and is probably a magical formula with no meaning in natural language. The bone was probably used as a tool in magic or divination.

Another purely magical inscription is found on an amber bead which was for a long time owned by a family in the town of Ennis in the Barrony Islands. The bead is said to have healing powers and to be of help in childbirth. The inscription which runs around the bead appears:

Macalister transliterates this: ATUCMLU. Which again would be an example of a purely magical formula in ogham fews.

But apparently not only small portable objects were inscribed with such formulas. There is also the example of the B side of the stone of Glenfahan (County Kerry, Ireland), which can be transliterated: LMCBDV – again a magical formula. The Christian motifs were probably carved on later in an attempt to exorcise the stone of its pagan power.

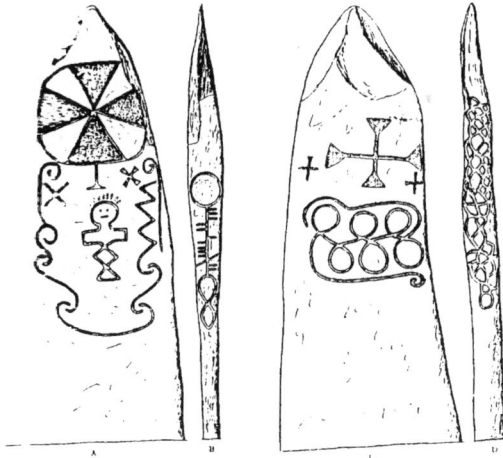

The Book of Ogham

Ogham in Early Irish Literature

It seems obvious that the writers of early Irish literature were familiar with ogham in the context they report on. However, by the time the sagas and laws were written down, the actual practice of carving ogham memorials had already died out. The literature is full of references, some perhaps intentionally unclear, regarding bygone beliefs and practices.

The most frequent reference to ogham in Old Irish literature corresponds exactly with what is most frequent in the archaeological record: memorial stones. Quite often in the tale of a great hero, his death scene will be concluded with a formulaic statement such as – scríbthair a ainm n-ogaim ("his name is written in ogham"). The verb used for "write" or "inscribe" is always O.Ir. scríbaid and the inscription is called ainm n-ogaim. The object onto which the characters are carved is referred to as either a lia "stone" or coirthe "rock". Characteristically there are also other ritual activities variously described in connection with this activity: e.g. "digging the grave", "setting the stone", "mourning the dead", and "observing funeral games". For more on this aspect see McManus (1991, pp. 154-155).

Besides these references to memorial or standing stones, there are some thirteen more problematic descriptions of the use of ogham. These are discussed by McManus (1991, 155-156). Each instance records ogham being used for some communicative process, but not all references are of the same quality. In the past some scholars were fond of describing some of these references to a magical use of ogham, while in more recent times the fashion has been to dismiss them as "having nothing to do with magic". -- Yet neither of these groups of scholars seem to have defined what they meant by the word "magic" in the first place. At the outset of our discussion let me define magic as: A technique by which a human being is able, by the power of volition, to affect events in subjective and/or objective reality, which given ordinary means would be impossible. Additionally, it is now widely thought that magic is essentially a semiotic or communicative process by which the will of an operator (i.e. "magician") is encoded and communicated to a causal agent which returns the communication in the form of phenomena which are in harmony with the willed communication of the magician. Armed with these definitions, we are better equipped to deal with the question of magic in connection with the ogham inscriptions and literary references to them.

The literature and epigraphical record is relatively poor in obviously and unambiguously magical messages. One of the most obvious references to the possible magical use of ogham is found in Lebor Ogaim, where we read:

> This is the first thing written in ogham, >⊤⊤⊤⊤⊤⊤⊤⊤; that is, B (birch) was written, and it was written to give a warning to Lug son of Ethliu with regard to his wife to protect her from being carried away into the sidhe. (The message was) seven Bs in one branch of birch: Your wife will be carried away from you seven times into the sidhe or into another country unless the birch guard her.

Clearly the belief is being expressed that the carving of ogham characters (by the right person, in the right way)can protect one from supernatural or otherwise perhaps malevolent forces or circumstances.

In the Irish prose literature there is a series of five intriguing references to ogham in connection with the divine hero CúChulainn. This is especially meaningful since one of the sets of ancient bríatharogaim, or kennings for the names of the ogham letters, is traditionally ascribed to this hero. (See below.) One of these references from the "Boyhood Deeds" (AIT p.147) describes how the youthful hero comes upon a pillar-stone around which is an "iron ring of heroic deeds" the peg (menoc) of which bears the following ogham inscription: "If any man came on the green, and if he were a warrior who bore arms, it was taboo (geis) for him to leave the green without challenging (someone) to single combat." The hero reads the message and responds by heaving the pillar-stone, ring and all, into the nearby water. This foolhardy act foreshadows CúChulainn's death. The three other references to ogham in connection with CúChulainn occur in texts treating events of the "Cattle-Raid of Cooley". Each time

31

The Book of Ogham

CúChulainn is shown to inscribe ogham inscriptions to delay the advance of the opposing army (and in one also to ensure time to tryst with his concubine). The fifth example of CúChulainn and ogham has him giving the king of Albu his little spear with an ogham inscription in it in exchange for a boat and a sea-charm from the king to aid him in a quest. The inscription will give the king leave to sit in CúChulainn's seat at Emain Macha, the capital of Ulster.

Two other references bear witness to the inscribing of ogham characters on four rods of yew wood. One of these, which occurs in a version of the "Wooing of Étaín", describes how a druid is able to divine the location of Étaín as he "makes four rods of yew and writes ogham in them and it is revealed to him by means of his keys of knowledge that Étaín is in the síd." This is the clearest attestation of the use of ogham for divinatory purposes and gives us the most technical details about how it was done. The other example which mentions the four rods of yew appears more ambiguous as a fili resorts to carving an incantation (O.Ir. díchetal) containing the names of the kings of Ireland down to the end of time on four such rods because it was too difficult to remember it without such an aid.

The other five attestations of ogham for such communicative purposes in Old Irish literature provide a mixed bag of information. In one Bran, upon his return from a voyage to the Land of Women, writes poetic stanzas describing that voyage in ogham before again sailing away from Ireland. (AIT, p. 595.) Another passage from the Book of Leinster describes how an ogham inscription carved in a shield indicates a specific fate of an individual and by changing either the interpretation or the inscription itself, the fate of the person bearing the shield will be changed. There are also two examples from the Senas Cormaic. One (entry 1018) is an example of ogham being used to make an indirect accusation of infidelity – this message is said to be carved into a four-sided rod (O.Ir. flesc cetharchuir). The other is a reference to the Old Irish word fé (entry 606) which is said to have been a rod of yew (O.Ir. flesc idaith) which was used in pagan graveyards to measure corpses and graves and which was said to have ogham writing on it. Lastly there is an elaboration on a biblical passage (II Samuel 11:14) where David sends a secret message to Joab

The Book of Ogham

to have Uriah the Hittite sent into the forefront of battle that he might be killed so that David can then have his wife Bathsheba. In the Irish version this message is said to be in "ogham".

As meagre as this evidence is, it does point to the belief that ogham was used for magical purposes. In one instance it is the medium for the declaration of a geis, a "magical taboo", in another it is unambiguously used for divinatory purposes, in several of the passages dealing with CúChulainn's use of ogham, it is said that inscriptions are somehow able to delay the advance of armies. In another instance an inscription is able to change someone's fate. While the legendary first ogham inscription is said to be intended as a protection against abduction into the síd-mound. Each of these show typical magical motives – some divinatory, some apotropaic, others more operative.

Ogham Tractates

No manuscripts actually written in ogham exist, although it has been thought that the "books" mentioned by Classical authors referred to such records written in ogham. This is not likely for reasons mentioned above about why the ancient bards and druids would not have wanted to commit their wisdom to writing. Additionally there is no evidence of ogham being used before the 4th century CE. The manuscripts we are talking about here are really medieval treatises explaining the use of ogham – such as the oldest and most famous one in the Book of Ballymote, which dates from the 1300s. There are a number of other manuscripts containing similar tracts on the use of ogham, but they all seem derived from the same source material collected by medieval antiquarians. These various manuscripts are discussed by G. Calder in his edition of the Auraicept na n-Eces.

On plate 1 I have reproduced a leaf from the Book of Ballymote (BB 313), showing many variant forms of ogham. It will be noticed that most of the long stem-lines going across the whole page contain two oghamic systems each.

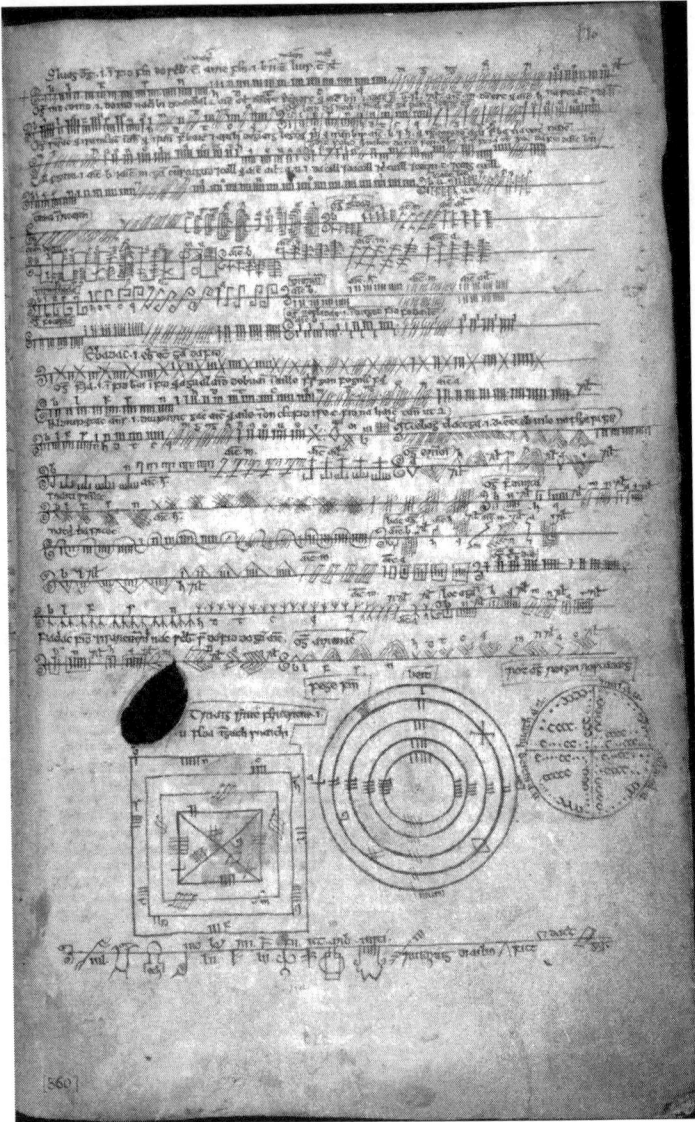

The Book of Ogham

These collections and the lore contained in the medieval Irish manuscripts are not magical uses of ogham as such, but they do reflect magical uses and practices of an earlier time. These practices were usually not very well understood by the scribes and scholars collecting the material, so it is no wonder that it often appears somewhat confused and bewildering.

It is very probable that the two figures at the bottom of the Book of Ballymote (leaf 313) called the "Stream Strand of Ferchertne" and "Finn's Wheel" were originally devices for the practice of magic and/or divination. Certainly they are partial cosmological maps which can be applied in these fields by those with knowledge (see chapter 2 for an unfoldment of the mystery of Finn's Window, for example).

The Irish Letter Names and the Mystery of Ogham

The ogham tractates and the manuscript tradition in general, although it stems from a later medieval tradition, does contain the evidence we need to reconstruct the original ogham system. This evidence comes in the form of the so-called bríatharogaim, or "word oghams". These are three lists of kennings, or circumlocutions, for the names of the ogham characters. It is these kennings that are the oldest evidence we have for the names of the ogham letters. Most recently, and most thoroughly, the question of their identity has been taken up by Professor Damien McManus (1988 and 1991). He has been able to identify the older names which predate the systematic replacements by purely tree or plant names which took place as part of a reformation of the system during the Middle Ages. First, I present the Old Irish originals, followed by modern English translations.

The Book of Ogham

	Bríatharogaim Morainn mac Moin	Bríatharogaim Maic ind Oc	Bríatharogaim Con Culainn
B	Fóchos foltchain	Glaisem cnis	Maise malach
L	Lí súla	Carae cethrae	Lúth cethrae
F	Airenach fían	Comét lachta	Dín cridi
S	Lí ambí	Lúth bech	Tosach mela
N	Costud síde	Bág ban	Bág maise
H	Condál cúan	Bánad gnúise	Ansam aidche
D	Ardam dosae	Grés soir	Slechtam soíre
T	Trian roith	Smiur gúaile	Trian n-airm
C	Caíniu fedaib	Carae blóesc	Milsem fedo
Q	Clithar baiscill	Bríg anduini	Dígu fethail
M	Tressam fedmae	Arusc n-airlig	Conar gotha
G	Milsiu féraib	Ined erc	Sásad ile
GG	Lúth lego	Étiud midach	Tosach n-échto
Z	Tressam rúamnai	Mórad rún	Saigid nél
R	Tindem rucci	Rúamnae drech	Bruth fergae
A	Ardam íachta	Tosach frecrai	Tosach garmae
O	Congnaid ech	Féthem soíre	Lúth fían
U	Uaraib adbaib	Sílad cland	Forbbaid ambí
E	Érgnaid fid	Commaín carat	Bráthair bethi
I	Sinem fedo	Caínem sen	Lúth lobair

The Book of Ogham

	Word Ogham of Morainn mac Moin	Word Ogham of Maic ind Oc	Word Ogham of Cú Chulainn
B	withered foot with fine hair	greyest of skin	beauty of the eyebrow
L	lustre of the eye	friend of cattle	sustenance of cattle
F	vanguard of the warrior-band	container of milk	protection of the heart
S	pallor of a dead man	sustenance of bees	beginning of honey
N	establishing of peace	boast of women	boast of beauty
H	assembly of packs of hounds	blanching of faces	most difficult at night
D	most exalted tree	handicraft of an artificer	most carved of craftsmanship
T	one of three parts of a wheel	marrow of coal	one of three parts of a weapon
C	fairest tree	friend of nutshells	sweetest tree
Q	shelter of a lunatic	substance of an insignificant person	dregs of clothing
M	strongest in exertion / most noble goodliness	proverb of slaughter	path of the voice
G	sweetest grass / greenest pasture	suitable place for cows	sating of multitudes
GG	sustenance of a leech	raiment of physicians	beginning of slaying
Z	strongest reddening	increase of secrets	seeking of clouds
R	most intense blushing	reddening of faces	glow of anger
A	loudest groan	beginning of an answer	beginning of a calling
O	wounder of horses	smoothest of craftsmanship	sustaining of warrior-bands
U	in cold dwellings	propagation of plants	shroud of a dead man
E	discerning tree	exchange of friends	brother of birch
I	oldest tree	fairest of the ancients	energy of an infirm person

37

The Book of Ogham

The original names of the ogham characters therefore clearly seem to have been as follows:

B	beithe	"birch-tree"
L	luise	"flame, radiance" and lus "plant, herb, vegetable"
F	fern	"alder-tree"
S	sail	"willow-tree"
N	nin	"forked branch" and "lofty"
H	úath	"fear, horror"
D	duir	"oak-tree"
T	tinne	"bar, rod of metal, ingot, mass of molten metal"
C	coll	"hazel"
Q	cert	"bush" and "rag"
M	muin	"neck" and "trick" and "love"
G	gort	"field"
GG	gétal	"(act of) wounding, slaying"
Z	straif	"sulphur"
R	ruise	"reddening"
A	ailm	"pine-tree" (?)
O	onn	"ash-tree"
U	úr, úir	"earth, soil; grave"
E	éo	"salmon" > edad "aspen"
I	éo	"yew-tree" > idad

For explanations of the linguistics behind the history of the letter names see McManus (1991, pp. 34-39). The last two letter-names require some explanation here, however. They are artificial creations of late origin which came about because the two names fell together linguistically, both being phonetically éo. The rhyming letter names seem to have been substituted later to avoid the confusion.

The objective study of these kennings reveals that the original system of ogham names had only seven, or possibly eight, tree or plant names, and that the rest had nothing to do with plants. Ogham was not originally a "tree alphabet". The lore surrounding these names adds tremendously to our wealth of information about the ogham ideology – and most especially about the ogham values from the stage

The Book of Ogham

of the tradition closest to pagan times.

The Role of Mystery in the Function of Ogham

The ogham system is enveloped in mystery. So it was from the beginning. The word "ogham" can be equated with written, as opposed to spoken, Irish. Names of the Irish letters (i.e. sounds) were the same, whether written as Roman or ogham characters. The use of the tally-oriented signary therefore can be seen to have had an encoding or encrypting function. One of the ogham systems in the Auraicept na n-Eces bears the name rúnogam na Fian: "secret ogham of the warrior-bands". This word rún (or rúine) in Old Irish, cognate with Germanic rún-, means "mystery" -- something hidden or occult. It translates Latin/Greek mysterium.

This word rúine and ogham share a common semantic destiny in the language, which is in itself revealing of deeper original affinities. Ogham develops the meaning of "idea, inference; intention". There is the adverbial phrase d' aon ogham, "intentionally" in Irish and Scots Gaelic oidhim, "intention, purpose". This semantic development stems from the intrinsically cryptic, secret nature of ogham. This is borne out by the close parallel in semantic development with the stem rún-. Rún, "secret", comes also to mean "secret thoughts, wishes", and hence "intention, purpose, design". From this it gains the associative meaning of "full consciousness, knowledge". A derivative word is also rúnid, "a confidant, counselor". Perhaps predictably from all this, the word rún also develops a meaning as a term of endearment – something like "darling, love". It should be noted that grammatically both rún and ogham are feminine.

From this it seems clear that the role of secrecy or mystery is essential to ogham at its core, and that more importantly the roots of consciousness – the very soil in which knowledge can grow – are to be found in the realm of encoded symbolic forms: ogham.

39

The Book of Ogham

The Legacy of the Ogham-Lore

It is most likely that the esoteric importance of ogham was in its prime in the "classical period" -- 4th-11th centuries - and that the time of the first great reform of the tradition - following the 11th century - was its first time of decline. Clearly the esoteric value of the tradition was still recognised and cultivated in this later period, but it was being progressively overwhelmed by the more international Latin symbolism as the Middle Ages wore on. Luckily some of the traditions surrounding ogham were recorded and preserved in medieval manuscripts.

Knowledge of ogham and its intricacies slowly died out in the Celtic realms. We know, for example, that the Earl of Glamorgan communicated with Charles I of England using ogham as a cipher in the early 1600s. But it seems that even for our Old Irish scholars of the early Middle Ages the real mysteries of the ogham were rapidly being lost.

The Puritan English invasion of Ireland in 1649 and the ensuing destruction of the independent Irish national culture almost put an end to the traditional oral transmission of lore from generation to generation.

It was not until the great and enthusiastic Celtic revival beginning in the 1700s that the ogham again began to get some attention as a system which perhaps encoded actual druidic wisdom. Unfortunately these inspired seekers did not yet have the science at their disposal - a science that would have been very much appreciated by the ancient druids - to unlock these mysteries. In the absence of science, often poetic fancy was substituted. Poetic fancy can be very effective when trying to conjure profound subjective experiences - many would-be magicians have been led astray by drugs in this regard. But for objective and eternal results the hard and steadfast knowledge and truth of the oak is needed.

Among the most important writers on the significance of ogham during this Romantic period was Roderic O'Flaherty. His book Ogygia, published in 1793, would later be used as a source book by Robert Graves in writing his work The White Goddess (1948).

The Book of Ogham

The importance of Graves' book is that it was widely read by adherents of the newly emerging witchcraft movement in Britain and America. The ogham-lore contained in the book thereby filtered into the neopagan world. Most subsequent works which even marginally touched on this topic heavily used material gleaned from Graves' widely available and popular book. The story of the revival of the esoteric utilisation of ogham is to a degree the story of the influence of this book and the gradual liberation of the field from the tyranny of its poetic subjectivism.

Perhaps the first widely available practical utilisation of ogham was represented by Liz and Colin Murray, whose divination-kit product was meant to be a Celtic rival to Ralph Blum's highly lucrative rune-kit. Unfortunately, this product was quite poorly researched and brought us no closer to a genuine esoteric revival.

In January of 1990 Edred Thorsson completed the manuscript of the work which was to become the first edition of The Book of Ogham. This was based on Edred's exoteric and esoteric researches of the late 1970s conducted when he was undertaking a course of study in Old Irish literature and language. Certainly, Edred's most significant contribution was not in the area of the lore of the individual ogham characters, but rather in the areas of Celtic psychology and especially cosmology as it relates to the ogham system.

Other major contributors to the current crop of esoteric ogham writings are John Matthews and Steven Blimires. Neither Matthews nor Blimires have quite been able to synthesise the current scholarship on ogham and liberate themselves from the influences of previous interpretations based on Graves and his Romantic predecessors.

The fact that the original ogham system was not based on purely tree names has come late to our understanding. This realisation has reopened doors closed, even in the latter day traditions, since the beginning of the system.

It has not been until recently that tools necessary to recover true and authentic ogham lore have been at our disposal again. Centuries of ignorance and prejudice imposed by Christian belief and lack of scholarly insight have had to be peeled away under the light of

The Book of Ogham

druidic science and analysis for the new dawn of the light emitting from within the síd to begin to shine again.

Chapter 2
Celtic Cosmology and Divination

The ogham fews, in their specific ordering of numbers and sounds, constitute a symbolic representation of the entirety of Celtic thought. In order to use them in divination – or in the more dynamic processes of magic – we need to learn to see the universe in the same way as those who devised these oghams as representations of universal truths. Until we can place the oghams fairly accurately within the context of their creators, we will fail to grasp their true meaning and purpose, and the subtle ways in which they interact will be lost to our perception.

In order to study ogham, therefore, we need to make a study of the cosmogony, cosmology, psychology and theology of the Celtic peoples who devised them in order to mirror their own patterns of thought and understanding. This will provide us with the structure underlying the oghams.

Cosmogony

Unlike other mythologies, we are not in possession of any straightforward, simple account of the Celtic creation myth, of how the

43

The Book of Ogham

world came into being. All other evidence indicates that the Celts must indeed have had a sophisticated notion of the emergence of the universe, but we will have to go back to the body of lore and start looking for ways to reconstruct it. We can discount the cosmological material of the so-called Barddas, a collection of Welsh manuscripts first created in the early 1800s by Iolo Morganwg and later published by J. Williams ab Ithel, as this is derived from Neo-Platonic ideas, not genuine Celtic lore.

A study of the available literature quickly reveals a tendency of the Celtic peoples to present their mythology as factual history, to write of gods and goddesses as if they were human beings. A great deal of fascinating speculation on the storyteller's art could be extrapolated from this, but this is not the time and place for that. Instead, we can simply be thankful that this process of historicising mythology probably saved some of the material we still have from Christian censorship.

A study of the Celtic tales indicates the importance of recurring patterns. The processes of coming-into-being recorded in these tales were assumed to be universal and by studying those which we have, we can isolate the key steps in the process of formation and manifestation as perceived by the ancient Celtic peoples. Once isolated, we can use these authentic keys to recreate something which must be very similar to the cosmology held by these people, and the process by which that cosmology came into being.

Given both the inclinations of the Irish and the importance of recurring patterns between greater and lesser manifestations, the land of Ireland can be viewed as symbolic of the entire world. If we trace the mythic principles underlying the development of Ireland, then we can apply these same principles to the creation and shaping of the entire world. In order to do this, we can analyse the pattern of shaping recorded in the Lebor Gabála Erenn (Book of the Invasions of Ireland). This book records that Ireland was invaded five times before the coming of the "Sons of Mil" (the Gaelic people). In this tale, we find ourselves presented with a process whereby an originally unshaped and empty land is defined and given substance through a series of five "invasions", or waves of manifestation. By examining the

44

The Book of Ogham

additional substance and being given to the land by each successive invasion, we can reconstruct a mythic cosmogony resonant with authentic Celtic thought. The invasions were as follows:

1. The people of Cessair lived on the land before the deluge and did not "divide" or shape it. Here we have the first undifferentiated manifestation of the world, substance as yet without shape or form, but carrying the potential for becoming.
2. The second invasion was that of the Partholon, who divided the land into four parts. In so doing, they created a flat plane with directions, on which life could emerge.
3. Third came the Nemed, who divided the land by three. In so doing, they added a vertical axis, the concepts of "above" and "below", allowing a spiritual dimension to permeate reality.
4. The fourth wave of invaders were the Fir Bolg, who divided the land into "fifths". This synthesised the four and the three into a new model of reality, symbolised by four quarters surrounding a centre.
5. Into this fully three dimensional manifestation came the fifth invasion, the Tuatha Dé Danann, who brought into the land an entirely new dimension of spirituality which defied the laws of the three dimensions already established and introduced a multidimensional consciousness of reality.

Finally came the Gaelic folk, who accepted the fivefold division of the Fir Bolg, but also divided the land into two halves, an upper and lower (north and south). This additional twofold division symbolises the duality which is prevalent throughout all of human existence – night and day, male and female, inside and outside, etc. (This is also interesting in light of the Celtic fascination with "in between" states, such as the twilight which is neither day nor night, or standing with one foot in water and another on land, neither of one realm nor the other; these "in between' times and places are important to the practice of Celtic magic, as those times when the ordinary dimensional limitations are transcended and the hidden dimensions made manifest by the Tuatha Dé Danann may be accessed by mortals.)

45

The Book of Ogham

Patterns of manifestation, and the successive waves of the ordering of things, were universal principles in the eyes of the Celts, and what was true of the structuring of Ireland with its invasions is also true of the formation of the ordered world out of chaos. We may never rediscover the actual creation myth of the ancient Gaelic peoples, but we can be quite confident that its several stages will be akin to those revealed in the ordering of the land of Ireland. In Indo-European ideology, every time a new land is taken, the world is recreated there. Thus we have our model of the Celtic cosmogony.

Cosmology

We are faced with a similar problem when trying to reconstruct a coherent model of Celtic cosmological thinking. Although the tales offer us innumerable accounts of the Otherworld, these accounts differ widely and we are given no overall plan to place them upon. The very nature of the heroic tales argues for the existence of a coherent and sophisticated system having been in place at one time, though. The heart and soul of a spiritual tradition lie in its cosmological and psychological lore, so perhaps it should come as no surprise to us that these factors are largely casualties of the Christian re-editing of the mythic material, whether through ignorance or malice. Fortunately, enough fragments remain for us to be able to reconstruct a coherent overview with the keys provided by modern comparative studies.

One of the first things the reader is struck with when reading the old Celtic tales is the imminence of the Otherworld; it breaks through into this world in many times and in many places, admitting the hero to its mysterious realms and denizens. The Otherworld may be seen as an other-dimensional reality, or an alternate universe, which lies very closely to our own familiar world, and the two may touch, overlap, or intertwine when the circumstances are right. An entrance may hide behind every door, around every corner, behind every hill; it is omnipresent.

There are actually three levels of worlds in Celtic cosmology,

46

The Book of Ogham

as the Otherworld and the Underworld are quite distinct and separate
from one another and the terms should not be used interchangeably.
The level we are most familiar with, our world of three dimensions in
space and motion (= time) is named bith. The term "Otherworld"
actually encompasses several distinct realms, all of which are
symbolically spoken of as being "higher" than our own world. It
possesses a different dimensional reality than our own world of three
dimensions, but exists in parallel. Although difficult to enter, its
hidden doorways may open into our world anywhere, as stated above.
The most usual gateways in tradition are burial mounds, sacred wells,
or trees. The third world, the Underworld, is symbolically very distant
from our own, and is spoken of as being located in the far west, or
under the sea.

Although the existing tales give us no accurate tally of the
number of worlds conceived by the Celts, we can reasonably assume
that they originally had a nine world system, since this number figures
so largely in their cosmology, and also in that of kindred Indo-
European cultures, such as the Germanic peoples. However, the
number five would also be of primary importance, being
representative of the provinces or fifths (O.Ir. coiced) into which all
territory was divided in the Irish scheme of thought. The pattern of
fifths is representative of four outer realms, surrounding a fifth (Mide)
in the mystical centre. This mystical centre is the gateway through
which the influence of the Otherworld enters into this world.

Although the forfedha, or "additional letters", were a belated
addition to the oghamic system, they do have a special significance
when considering Celtic cosmology. As latecomers to the system of
writing, they stand somewhat outside it. Moreover, they have a
completely different look to the other ogham characters. The shapes
of the forfedha are of a genuinely symbolic appearance rather than just
a tally, and these shapes are suggestive of their cosmological and
divinatory significance. The shape of each forfedha can be seen to
correspond in meaning to one of the fifths, and the forfedha when
taken as a whole can therefore be arranged in the pattern of the fifths
as a complete cosmological map, which may be incorporated into the
design of the casting cloth. This is tabulated below.

47

The Book of Ogham

Represented by crossed lines, the ea-few is symbolic of the absolute centre and is placed right in the middle of the diagram, representative of the mystical centre, with the other fifths arranged around it. See table 2.1 below for a complete list of the cosmological meanings of the fifths and the attributions of the forfedha.

TABLE 2.1 The Cosmological Meanings of the Forfedha

Shape	Sound	Direction	Field	Meaning
⊱▦	ae	east	blath	manifestation
⊱✖	io	north	cath	conflict - resistance
⊱◠	ui	west	fis	learning – spiral
⊱◇	oi	south	seis	harmony – space
⊱✕	ea	centre	mide	middle – focus

This arrangement of fifths is diagrammatically represented in figures 2.1 and 2.2 below.

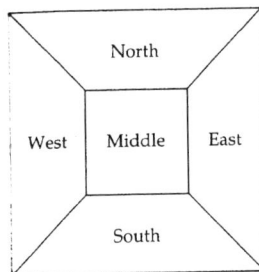

Figure 2.1 The Fifths

The Book of Ogham

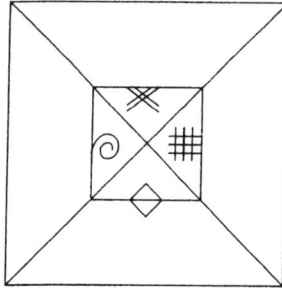

Figure 2.2 The Forfedha in the Fifths

The forfedha can be seen to describe an unfolding spiral, which commences at the X point in the middle (the ea-few) and leads to an open space (the oi-few)in which manifestation can take place, through a spiral or cyclical motion (the ui-few), which produces friction through resistance and conflict (the io-few), which brings into being the completed matrix of manifestation in the grid pattern of the world (the ae-few).

Having established this basic coherent model of Celtic cosmology, and through careful analysis of the names given to the various Otherworlds and Underworlds in Celtic mythology, it is possible to reconstruct a complete cosmological system that probably comes very close to the original conception. In reconstructing the worlds upon this planar model, the term magh (plane) has generally been given to the supernal Otherworlds, while the term tír (Land) has been given to the realms of the Underworld.

The Otherworld as a whole can be called by the Old Irish name Magh Mor, meaning the Great Plane, while the Underworld can be called by the name Tír Andomain, meaning the Land of the Un-World, or Anti-World. Between these two realms lies this world (Bith). In accord with the model of fifths already established, each of these three realms of reality can be subdivided into four outer provinces surrounding a centre. Magh Mor is divided into four realms indicative of (1) age, (2) light, (3) abundance and (4) happiness,

49

while Tír Andomain is divided into four realms indicative of (1) youth, (2) love, (3) vitality and (4) death. All of these influences flow into Bith through the mystical centre. These realms are tabulated in table 2.2.

TABLE 2.2 The Realms in Celtic Cosmology

The Upper- or Otherworld (Magh Mor)

	Name	Translation of Name	Quality
1	Sen Magh	Old Plain	(age)
2	Magh Findargat	Plain of White Silver	
	Magh Imchiunn	Plain of Extreme Gentleness	(light)
	Magh Argetnel	Plain of Silver Clouds	
3	Magh Mell	Plain of Delight	
	Magh Airctbech	Plain of Bounty	(abundance)
	Magh Ildathach	Plain of Many Colours	
4	Magh Ionganaidh	Plain of Wonder	(happiness)

The Middle World (Bith of Mide)

The Under- or Anti-World (Tír Andomain)

	Name	Translation	Quality
1	Tír na n'Og	Land of Youth	(growth)
2	Tír fo Thuinn	Land Under the Wave	(death)
	Tech Duinn	House of Donn	
3	Tír na mBan	Land of Women	(love)
4	Tír na mBeo	Land of Life	(vitality)

It should be noted that one of the common names for the Underworld, Tír Tairngiri (the Land of Promise – or the "Promised Land"), has been ignored for our purposes of reconstructing the

The Book of Ogham

Celtic conception of cosmology, due to its obvious borrowing from the Christian tradition.

Having reconstructed this network of realms and worlds, it can be seen to resemble a tree, with branches and roots. Thus an entire support structure for the system of worlds, realms and provinces can be diagrammatically represented as in figure 2.3.

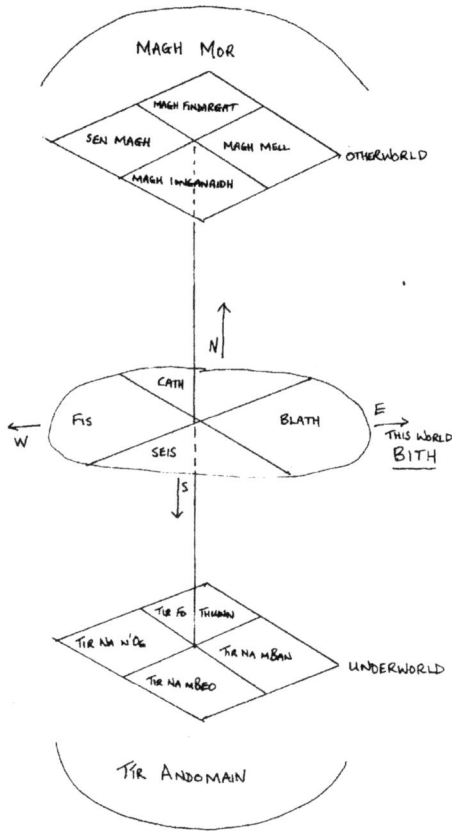

Figure 2.3 The Celtic Cosmology

The Book of Ogham

From this diagrammatic representation, we can construct a network of paths or streams which interconnect these realms and worlds. It should come as no surprise that these paths can be seen to be 20 in number: the same as the number of fews of the ogham system. Perhaps we are beginning to understand why the Celts viewed trees as gateways to other-dimensional realities!

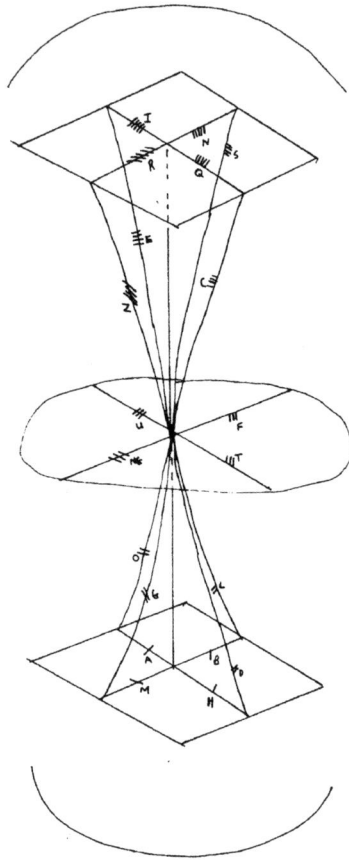

Figure 2.4 The Ogham Fews in the Celtic Cosmology

The Book of Ogham

The Oghamic Reflection in the Cosmos

In The Book of Ballymote we find a diagram called Finn's Window. The meaning behind this figure becomes obvious when it is applied as a key for understanding Celtic cosmology in accordance with oghamic principles. Finn's Window consists of five rings, each of which is inscribed with four ogham characters. If this two-dimensional Window model is projected into a three-dimensional figure, then the five groups of ogham fews can be seen to form the levels of the cosmic tree, as shown in figure 2.4.

In this way, the ogham fews are ascribed to each of the twenty paths of the cosmological scheme. The single stroke fews belong to the Underworld plane; the double stroke fews belong to the paths running between this world and the Underworld; the triple stroke fews belong to the everyday world, the material plane of existence; the quadruple stroke fews are the paths running from here to the Otherworld; finally, the quintuple stroke fews belong to the plane of the Otherworld itself.

The central axis of the diagram does not itself make up any of these paths. The various paths represent the means of human access to other-dimensional realities, but the vertical axis is the means whereby the influences of the Otherworlds flow through into this world.

Referring to the cosmological map depicted in figure 2.3, it will be noted that there are symbolic directions indicated. These directions are derived from the four "Otherworldly cities" of Irish tradition. The cities are represented as existing on all three levels of being simultaneously, which is indicative of the universality of the states of being symbolised by these cities throughout the entire cosmos. The names, symbolic locations, masters and symbols are listed in table 2.3. It should be noted that the "masters" are clearly a later Christian addition.

The Book of Ogham

TABLE 2.3 The Otherworldly Cities

Name	Direction	Master	Symbol
Falias	North	Morfessa	Stone
Gorias	East	Esras	Spear
Finias	South	Uscias	Sword
Murias	West	Semias	Cauldron

In this Celtic cosmological scheme, we therefore find nine realms, which are arranged through three worlds, divided into a total of twelve provinces – all interconnected by twenty paths or streams. The universe can be seen to have essentially three levels of being, each level being divided into "fifths", i.e. a hidden or invisible centre surrounded by the external provinces.

If we now work in reverse, and re-project this scheme onto a flat surface in order to provide a map appropriate for the purpose of divination or the playing of sacred games intended to mirror the possible happenings within the whole cosmos, we find that the pattern of the "fifths" emerges, on which the divinatory cloth is based. It will be seen that this whole cosmic scheme is also the pattern which underlies the so-called Celtic cross.

Theories of Divination

We can define divination as the art and science of gaining hidden knowledge, especially when it is derived from divine or objective sources. Historically, the Celts used many different methods of divination, the oghams being just one of these many ways used to divine the hidden reality behind the world of appearances. Unfortunately, most of the other methods used are too obscure for us to be able to reconstruct them in any kind of accurate or reliable fashion. The ogham system, however, is well enough documented and enough of its true symbolism has survived intact for us to

The Book of Ogham

understand the essence of how it might have worked. This understandin has been applied in reconstructing Celtic cosmology for this chapter and has been put into practice in the system of ogham divination presented in this book.

It should be understood from the outset that true divination bears very little resemblance to popular notions of fortune telling. As the name itself implies, divination is a divine process, hence a sacred process. The aim of divination is to set up a meaningful dialogue with the universe – this to be interpreted as both the personal universe within the inquirer and the shared universe without. Divination is a way of learning things which would otherwise be hidden from the awareness of the inquirer. It should be understood that this knowledge may just as easily relate to the roots of things – the hidden history of a person or place – as it may to as yet unseen branches in the "yet to be". The ancient Indo-Europeans intuitively understood that the future or fate of a person or place is strongly linked to the past of that person or place. By fully and deeply understanding the influence of the past, we may learn to predict the future with considerable accuracy.

If we refer to the Old Irish literature, we find several references to the vital necessity of knowing the history of Ireland as a prerequisite to other knowledge. For example, we read in the Book of Invasions of the primeval figure Fintan son of Bochra (= Ocean), daughter of Bith (= World), who survived the primeval flood by living in the shape of a salmon and who was summoned to recount the history of Ireland so that the men of Ireland would know how to divide the land rightly. This "salmon of knowledge" is a recurring theme in Celtic lore. It symbolises the primeval understanding of the basis of existence. It is knowledge of this seed principle which makes all further knowledge possible.

In order for divination to be relevant and to be considered in any way "true" or "real", it must ultimately be derived from objective sources. The reason for stressing the necessity of establishing an authentic and accurate insight into Celtic tradition, cosmology and psychology is in order to establish an objective yardstick against which ogham divination may be measured. Without taking the trouble to engage in such research, anybody with a little imagination could easily recreate a seemingly Celtic means of divination; there is nothing easier in the world than for people to delude themselves into believing they have gained profound knowledge through purely subjective means. By taking the time and trouble to painstakingly recreate a genuine Celtic cosmological scheme, this pitfall may be avoided, as we are provided with an objective standard by which to measure our insights, something which does not derive from ourselves along. The ancients understood this well, which is why they were always so insistent on the derivation of their knowledge from true primeval sources. We today must be no less diligent if we wish to find true mysteries on our chosen paths.

Divination may be subdivided into two main types, an objectified type and a subjective type. As in all systems in which meaning is derived, both are essentially made up of symbol systems which are synthesised to arrive at a given meaning.

Examples of the objectified systems would be those connected to the runes, tarot, astrology and so forth. In these systems, one set of symbols (for example the planets in astrology) are juxtaposed or laid over another set of symbols (such as the zodiacal signs and houses in astrology). When using the tarot cards or the runes, picked symbol systems are laid down according to a symbolic pattern, and meaning is then derived from which symbol falls in each symbolic location and their relations with each other. Such systems take an essentially rational approach to the subject, and from this firm rational basis intuitive skill is then applied to interpret the symbols – their meaningful melding – in the final reading.

The best modern example of the subjective method of divination can be seen in the currently fashionable practice of "channeling". In this technique the diviner attempts to meld his / her mind with an inner (or outer) source of information. Within the Germanic school this method was known as seith, and among the Irish similar techniques were known as imbas forosna (inspiration from the knowledge of the masters) and dichetal do chennaib (composing on the fingertips) or extemporary incantation. Perhaps the best known surviving Celtic example of the subjective method of divination - albeit coming down to us in a very late form - would be the Prophecy of Merlin, contained in Geoffrey of Monmouth's Histories of the Kings of Britain.

In virtually all kinds of divination, therefore, we see that two systems of meaning are synthesised and brought together to result in an expanded interpretation of the symbols which go beyond the obvious into some otherwise hidden realm of significance. This process should not be as extraordinary as it might first appear on the surface. After all, our everyday language and its common understanding is based upon the same principle; it has simply become second nature to us. We use words, which are placed in certain meaningful positions in a context (sentence) in order to derive some meaning from the words. Each word has a meaning in its own right, but in the overall context of the sentence it acquires more significance and may sometimes change its meaning entirely based upon where it appears in a given sentence and in relation to which other words.

In many ways, the symbolic systems of divination work on the same principles as those used in natural languages, but they signify something beyond the ordinary, natural systems. Divinatory symbols must be interpreted by a higher faculty of the soul in order for them to be reliably used. In using a divinatory metalanguage, the Bards are virtually having conversations with their environment.

With the ogham system, the ogham fews constitute the "words" of the metalanguage, while the various patterns found in the cosmic order expressed in the cosmological maps used in the various layouts maker up their "sentences", or contexts in which these complex symbols can be understood and interpreted.

The Celtic View

In the Celtic world, ogham is not the only kind of divination known. Although the ogham system is the focus of this book, by looking at the other kinds of Celtic divination we will certainly better understand the nature and uses of the oghamic form, and the perspective with which it was applied.

The Book of Ogham

In the ancient Celtic sources, there are many different methods mentioned for gaining hidden knowledge. There were methods involving the induction of prophetic dreams, as well as those for drawing out inspired utterances of prophecy from the bard through poetry. Those readers who practice the curriculum of study suggested in this book will indeed become very familiar with the magical and divinatory applications of alliterative poetry.

The induction of prophetic dreams is known in Old Irish by such terms as tarbfeis ("bull feast") and taghairm. The tarbfeis involved the eating of the flesh and drinking the blood of a correctly sacrificed bull and sleeping wrapped up in its still warm hide. This was done with the special purpose of inducing a dream to determine the identity of the future king. The taghairm simply had the diviner wrapped up in the warm hide of a freshly sacrificed ox. The seer then slept in this hide in a remote location until prophetic dreams were induced.

In a work called "Cormac's Glossary" (Sanas Cormaic) we read of three distinct types of divination practised by the ancient Irish: imbas forosnai ("revelation of knowledge"), teinem laida ("cracking [or analysis] of a poem"), and dichtetal do chennaib ("extemporary incantation").

The imbas forosnai involves the chewing of raw meat of a sacrificial animal. The meat is offered to the gods while incantations are sung over the diviner's hands. The diviner then goes to sleep covering his eyes with his hands - the right palm over the left eye, and the left palm over the right eye. The dreams will reveal the desired knowledge.

Teinm laida, like imbas forosnai, was connected with sacrifice and the old gods of the people. For this reason both were strictly prohibited by the Christians. With "cracking open" or analysis of a situation poetically, the diviner composes a poetic work to find the answer to a question.

The form of divination called dichtetal do chennaib is apparently based on the mind and abilities of the diviner alone with no outside help from the gods or sacrificial acts.

One recurring ritual element in the Celtic tradition is that of the det fis – the Tooth of Knowledge, which is said to be possessed by Finn mac Cumhaill. In one story, he gets his thumb caught in a door jamb, and in another he touches his thumb to a cooking salmon ("the Salmon of Knowledge"). In both cases, he puts the injured digit in his mouth to relieve the pain and is suddenly gifted with prophetic insight. This is paralleled in the Saga of the Volsungs in the Germanic tradition, where we read of Sigurd gaining divinatory powers when he burns his finger on the bubbling heart-blood of the serpent Fafnir, and similarly puts his finger in his mouth. In these cases, it is the magical connection to the praeterhuman realm (embodied in the salmon or serpent), coupled with a spontaneous, synchronistic "accident", which provides the impetus for the new unfoldment of powers.

Since the oghams are first and foremost a system of classifying and cataloguing in a complete and significant way all aspects of the world and environment, to the traditional Celtic mind the oghams would make up a complete set of symbols existing within and encompassing the natural cosmic order. To read where and how these aspects are working at any one time in a person's life is one of the chief things such a system makes possible. To continue with our linguistic analogy, the complete ogham system is the dictionary, while the cosmology is the grammar of the metalanguage. This goes a long way towards explaining the true significance of why the treatises on ogham go on and on about the various "kinds" of ogham. It is simply an effort to expand and refine the "dictionary" of symbolic meanings in order that the universe might be more accurately understood and interpreted.

In ogham, language itself is imbued with hidden meaning. In the original tradition, ogham was a science of language, and language was seen as a magical way to interact with the cosmos. Ogham divination as outlined here is the uncovering of the basic principles in this system and their use in a meaningful dialogue between the self and the world.

The Book of Ogham

Chapter 3
Celtic Psychology

The Soul

The successful practice of divination is dependent upon accurate analysis of the relationship existing between the individual and the world. In the previous chapter, we painstakingly reconstructed a model of the outer world, the objective universe. If we are to formulate a complete picture, we now need to turn our attention to the structure of the inner world, the subjective reality of the individual. This necessitates a study of Celtic lore concerning the human psyche, or soul.

It will be understood that all of our comprehension of the objective world surrounding us is filtered through our own senses and interpreted according to the subjective overlay of our own minds. Following on from our discussion of Celtic cosmology in the previous chapter, we can assume that there are also certain resonant patterns within the inner, subjective world which correspond to the patterns of the outer, objective world. Since all that we perceive and interpret is actually only seen through our own subjective lens, it follows that in order to use divination correctly to read the patterns coming into objective manifestation - or in order to use magic to establish certain desired patterns - we must have a clear comprehension of how the subjective and objective worlds interface with each other, otherwise we

The Book of Ogham

will be led astray. Even modern science is beginning to recognise the influence of the observer upon an experiment. A clear understanding of Celtic psychology in the interpretation of ogham is therefore every bit as important as the cosmological patterns.

It may come as a bit of a blow to the pride of modern men and women to have to face up to the fact that the ancient Celtic peoples had a much more complex and intricate understanding of the human soul than we do today. In common with the other Indo-European peoples, the Celts isolated and identified several distinct faculties which are today generally lumped together in such terms as "mind", "soul", "spirit", "psyche". etc. The interchangeability of these latter terms in modern parlance, and the ease with which any one of them can be substituted for another, is indicative of the paucity of our contemporary soul lore. The blame for this can be laid squarely at the feet of the Christian church, who belittled and condemned the human soul as a worthless thing, blameworthy in the eyes of their God.

The Celts used symbolic names to identify the various different aspects of the soul of which they had experience. These names were poetic in nature, intended to accurately convey the qualities inherent in the distinct "layers" of the composite human selfhood. These several distinct aspects of the soul are as follows:

1. The appearance or shape (delbh)
2. The elements (duile) which make up the body
3. The animating principle or breath (anál)
4. The mind and will (menma)
5. The memory (cuimhne)
6. The self (féin)
7. The shadow or shape-shifting form (púca or scal)
8. The shade or soul (enaid)

Therefore, when we interpret a reading of the ogham fews, what we are actually trying to do is read the interaction between these faculties of the soul and the outside world, and determine the possibilities inherent within that interaction.

The Book of Ogham

To discuss these parts of the soul in greater detail:

1. The delbh [delv] is not, as might be expected, the actual physical form of the individual, but is the shaping influence which determines how that physical form will manifest itself through its elements (duile – see below). The delbh is the aspect or image projected by the personality, that appearance of ourselves which we display to others. Good actors are very adept at manipulating the delbh so that they can project a completely different image of themselves depending upon what role they are playing. The delbh is a much more subtle vehicle than mere physical appearance and can be taken to encompass that aspect of the self which places an image of ourselves in the perceptions of others. As such, it is a malleable and manipulable (indeed, manipulative) aspect.

2. The duile [duiluh] are the six elements of the manifest human entity, making up the physical vehicle. These elements correspond to the elements which go to make up the world outside of self. They are as follows:

Human Element	World Element
anál (breath)	gaeth (wind)
imradud (mind)	nel (cloud)
drech (face)	grian (sun)
fuil (blood)	muir (sea)
colaind (flesh)	talamh (earth)
cnaimh (bone)	cloch (stone)

These elements are arranged in a descending order of density. The presence of the vital breath and mind in this list of bodily elements indicates the Celtic understanding of the interface between the physical and spiritual worlds in the mind-body complex.

3. The anál [anahl] is listed as part of the duile, but must also be considered as a separate aspect in its own right, because of its importance as the vital principle. It is the principle whereby the

63

life-force itself flows through the body and soul, animating them. It is also the principle of vitality whereby the "presence" of the individual may reach beyond the fleshy envelope and influence the world outside of self. It is neither an intellectual nor a physical force in its own right (though it finds its expressions in both); it is dynamic vitality, pure and simple.

4. The menma is both the active and the passive mental qualities, cognition and will combined. It is the whole process of thought and decision making. It incorporates the taking in and analysis of information, the application of that information to each situation, and the action of the will in consequence of that information. This is the part of the self which collects and processes data, emotionally as well as intellectually, then determines what action is appropriate. It is interesting that both the active and passive cognitive faculties are viewed in the Celtic scheme as a single function, the implication being that action without thought is detrimental to the overall balance of the soul, as is data-gathering without purpose.

5. The cuimhne [kuv-nuh] is the faculty of memory. As such, it involves the processes of pattern recognition and the association of ideas, things which are of tremendous importance to the aspiring bard. Only when the ogham fews can truly be said to live and interact within the cuimhne can true facility with the art be claimed.

6. The féin [fane] is the sense of self within an individual, it is the focal core through which all of the other psychological aspects are channeled and balanced to create a sense of coherent wholeness (or such at least is the ultimate aim. To become skilled in reading and interpreting the oghams – and thus in understanding yourself and the world around you – can induce a far greater degree of coherence and harmony in your life and selfhood than may otherwise have been the case.) It is through the féin that your consciousness expresses itself in the world, and expresses the world to itself. The féin is the open doorway to that part of you which is immortal.

7. The púca [pooka] is the most unsettling and disturbing part of the

psyche. It is that shadow-self which lurks beneath the threshold of consciousness and accompanies our every thought and deed. It is the home not only of deliberately repressed thoughts and inclinations, but also to those impulses which may be perfectly harmless ordinarily, but which we are too bound by conditioning and convention to give expression to. It can thus be a hotbed for neuroses if not properly managed. The oghams may be used to carefully explore and remould the psyche, laying bare the nature of the púca, integrating and accepting what is found there, bringing it into the personality in a balanced way, thus laying the potential 'dark side' to rest. When integrated, the púca may be energised to form several different 'personas', crafted to deal most efficiently with life's various situations. This is similar to when someone will say "I've got my accountant's hat on today" if they're dealing with the household bills. The púca can be energised to make such switches of aptitude easily. It can be either a powerful tool or a spectre of fear and denial.

8. The enaid [inathe] may be termed the 'shade' of a person, that which remains behind to carry forward the person's work and experience when an individual dies. It may speak through the memories of others who knew the person, or it may be seen as a ghost. For the duration of its existence, it retains some connection to the core consciousness of the person who has passed on, fading when this consciousness passes on to be reborn.

Figure 3.1 overleaf illustrates the way in which these faculties of the soul interact with each other to create the overall whole which is the individual. A good working understanding of Celtic psychology is important not only to gain historical perspective on how our forebears lived and thought, but also to make best use of our own psychic faculties when reading or otherwise manipulating the ogham fews.

The Book of Ogham

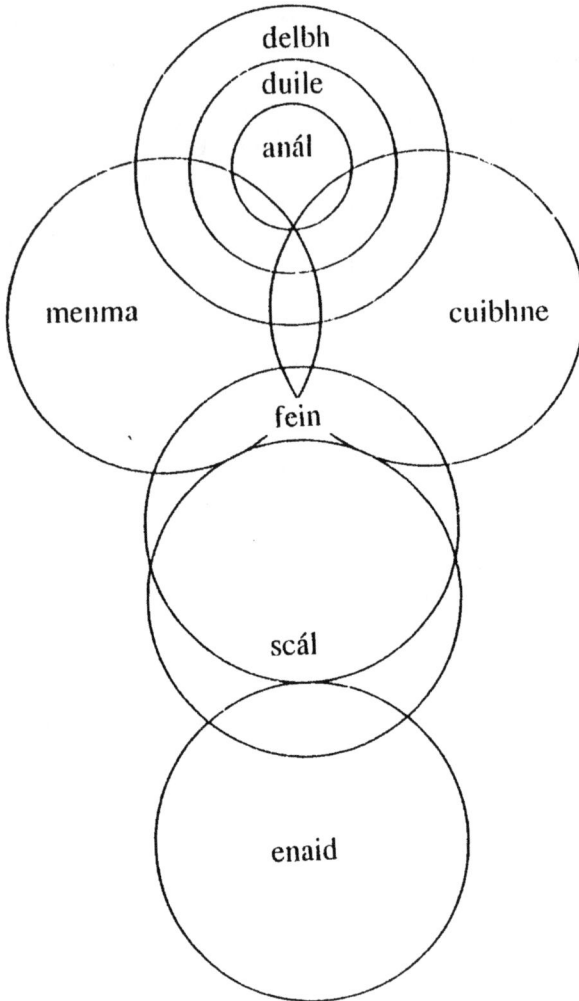

delbh

duile

anál

menma

cuibhne

fein

scál

enaid

Figure 3.1 Diagram of the Celtic Soul Concept

66

The Book of Ogham

Rebirth of the Soul

It is often glibly stated that the ancient Celtic peoples believed in reincarnation. This statement is in need of serious qualification, as the popular contemporary understanding of reincarnation is very far removed from the soul lore of the Celts. Think of all the times you have heard people casually discussing the possibility of reincarnation. Inevitably, one of the first questions asked will be, "What do you want to come back as?" or "Who do you want to come back as?" Even those with a less trivial and more thoughtful perspective on reincarnation will still generally hold that the soul can reincarnate as an animal, or as an individual in a completely different culture. The Celtic concept had very little relationship to this.

The ancient Celts possessed a much more integrated view of the soul-body concept than most people do today. As the bodily heritage was passed down to one's descendants genetically, so would the soul be reborn within the same cultural matrix, the same extended family group. In other words, the reincarnating soul would return to those influences and that environment which had shaped it, which it was already attuned to. It would be reborn within its own people.

It is interesting to examine figure 3.1 and the parts of the soul in the light of this belief, and to question what it is that is actually reborn. The enaid, the shade, is that part of the individual which carries the life force after death. It may have access to the memory and some degree of cognition, depending upon the unfulfilled goals which drive it. Much of the experience and wisdom of the individual will be passed on to the descendants in general through the enaid by a kind of spiritual osmosis. Those parts of the soul directly dependent upon the physical form - the duile - will of course atrophy. It is probably only actually the féin - the sense of Self itself, and the window upon the eternal core of consciousness - which truly passes on into a new life. This is why it becomes important to gain conscious control and integration of every part of the psyche, so that it becomes a harmonious whole. In this manner, a portion of the menma and the cuimhne - will and memory - may be successfully carried over along with the féin from one life to the next. I would also hazard that it

The Book of Ogham

might be possible to retain the delbh, the shaping principle, and thus carry ever greater proportions of the personality through into new manifestation.

So yes, the Celts were believers in reincarnation, but it was not an automatic process, nor was it as random as popularly believed by contemporary folk, and an examination of Celtic psychology makes it apparent that the several parts of the psyche each go their appointed way upon death. No knowledge or experience is ever truly lost, and it is always available to the descendants (and thus to the reborn individual) in one form or another. How much is actually retained as "property" of the reincarnated individual depends upon the degree of integration and self-awareness within the psyche.

The Greek ethnographer Poseidonios was probably the original source for most of the early classical references to the Celtic belief in immortality, equating the Celtic doctrine with that of the Greek philosopher Pythagoras. Poseidonios was probably Julius Caesar's source when he wrote the following passage in De Bello Gallico:

> A lesson which they [the druids] take particular pains to inculcate is that the soul does not perish, but after death passes from one body to another; they think this is the best incentive to bravery, because it teaches men to disregard the terrors of death.

Other classical authors – including Diodorus Siculus, Strabo and Lucanus – also wrote concerning the Celts' belief in immortality and rebirth. Their prime motive in doing so seems in each instance to be to explain the Celts' fearlessness in battle.

The most valuable direct evidence we have for Celtic belief, however, comes from the earliest literature of Ireland, Scotland and Wales, coupled with an examination of those cultures most closely akin to the Celts.

There are three main tales of rebirth in Irish literature: those of Etain, CúChulainn and Finn.

In the Etain cycle, we find what is perhaps the best example of the concept, because the tale spans three generations of rebirths. The third of these is the daughter of the second, and they all bear the same name. On the surface, this can seem somewhat confusing to the reader of these tales – but the meaning conveyed is most profound. Originally Etain is divine. She is the wife of the god Midir in the sídhe-mound (or Otherworld). Subsequently, she is incarnated as Etain, the daughter of Etar, king of Echrad. In this form, she marries Eochaid, king of Tara. Etain, the wife of Eochaid, then bears one daughter, also named Etain.

The CúChulainn cycle presents us with a classic example off the divine ancestor. After an interlude of three years in the Otherworld, Dechtire bears a son named Setanta. The god Lugh is the actual father of the boy, although Sualtagh, the mortal husband of Dechtire, claims him.

CúChulainn always remains conscious of his divine origin. This motif is the most common found in the Irish rebirth tales – a divine member of the Otherworld and one of the Tuatha Dé Danann is the father or mother of a "mortal" child and at the same time is thought to be "incarnated" in the child. (This follows from the basic idea that the descendants are the ancestors reborn.) Of course, the god continues to exist in the Otherworld while his "avatar" (to use a Sanskrit word for a similar conception) acts in this world.

The CúChulainn cycle also provides an example of another feature of the Celtic rebirth ideology separate from the influence of the Otherworld. In the tale called "The Wooing of Emer", CúChulainn's countrymen (the Ulstermen) are anxious that their champion and hero marry and produce an heir as soon as possible because of their fear that he would perish early. They wished for this heir "knowing that his rebirth (O.Ir. aithgain) would be of himself". This can easily be compared to the third rebirth of Etain.

The third primary example of this teaching in Irish literature is found in the "Voyage of Bran" and other later Irish tales dealing with Mongán. King Fiachna is out on warring expeditions when his wife is visited by a "noble looking man", who tells her that she should bear him a son in order to save her husband's life. The next morning before leaving he spoke this verse:

The Book of Ogham

I go home.
The pure pale morning draws near:
Manannán son of Lir
Is the name of him who came to thee.

Mongán was born from their union. It is also implied that Mongán is a rebirth of Finn mac Cumaill, "though he would not let it be told."

A fourth cycle involving the rebirth teaching is that of Finn mac Cumaill. Here we find the motif of the posthumous son who becomes a great hero. Cumaill is killed in battle, leaving his wife pregnant with his seventh son. When the boy is born, he is secretly fostered and nurtured in a remote forest area. Later, the king of Bantry, into whose service he anonymously enters, says: "If Cumaill had left a son one would think that thou (Finn) wast he. However, we have not heard of his leaving a son..." This motif is easily seen in the Mabinogi tale of "Peredur", and in its later development, "Parzival", it is even more apparent. A Germanic parallel can be found in the saga of Sigurd.

By taking these Irish uses as the most authentic evidence relating to the Celtic idea of rebirth, we are now in a position to consider whether or not the Celtic notion was indeed similar to that of the Pythagoreans. The Pythagorean doctrine tended to view the body with disdain, in their eyes it was a prison for the soul. Theirs was also a highly moralistic perspective, which led them to the belief that the soul would be reborn in circumstances reflective of the moral calibre of the previous life. Fine, upstanding citizens would thus be reborn in much better circumstances than unrepentant criminals. It is apparent that the Pythagoreans believed that the soul could transmigrate directly into any suitable vehicle being born at the time of its demise. It is unclear whether or not the Pythagoreans believed that human beings could be reborn in the bodies of animals.

By way of contrast, the Celtic doctrine of rebirth was not moralistic. Instead, it was intensely vitalistic. Rebirth was attained by gods, goddesses and heroes by their own inherent vitality and dynamism. Also, as discussed earlier in this chapter, the Celts were not at all disdainful of the body, seeing it as part of a vital, integrated mind-body complex. Indeed, to them rebirth into this world was not a prison, but a thing of joy, something to be greatly desired. Any similarity with the Pythagorean notion, therefore, was superficial. It seems much more likely that the Celts were continuing the rebirth beliefs common to the Indo-European peoples.

One feature which is especially emphasised within the Celtic tales is that the gods – the Tuatha Dé Danann – can have children with humans, giving birth to great mortal heroes who carry within them all the qualities of their Otherworldly sire. This idea carries forward even as late as the Arthurian tales, where Merlin is said to be only half human, having an Otherworldly father.

A more common theme is that of the rebirth of dead ancestors in their own descendants. In this process, the soul is reborn in the flesh of a newborn descendant. Unlike the Pythagorean belief, however, the soul will dwell in the Underworld between incarnations, awaiting the correct configuration of time and flesh and blood before being reborn to new life. Whilst in the Underworld, it may still make new commitments and undertake new obligations, some of which may be carried over into the new life.

Does a soul ever stop incarnating? It may be that as a soul gains more experience, its desire or need for rebirth may become less frequent (at least as we measure time; it is evident from the tales that time can pass at very different rates in the Underworld), or may even cease altogether. However, in spite of the delights to be found in the lands of Tír na mBan and Tír na mBeo, the pioneering drive and vitality of the Celtic spirit seem so strong that life in this world will always remain something to be desired.

The Book of Ogham

The Book of Ogham

Chapter 4
Interpretation of Oghams

This chapter forms the "raw material" to assist in understanding the meaning, interpretation and operative use of each of the ogham fews. With increased familiarity through intensive practice, you will in time gain your own personal perspective upon the oghams, and your divinations and thoughts will be informed by the best informational resource of all: your own intuitive link with and understanding of the principles underlying ogham. This level of proficiency is dearly bought with time and effort, however, and this chapter is designed to give you as much information as possible to set your work on the right footing at the very beginning, easing you into an operative understanding of the oghams as fluidly and smoothly as possible until that moment is reached when the outer symbols awaken as inner realities.

The oghams are here referred to by their restored original names, as discussed in chapter 1. Use of these names takes us one step closer to rediscovering the true insights of the druids and bards of old.

Each ogham is described under the following headings, which when taken together should provide you with an intuitive grasp of the principle of each few:

The Book of Ogham

Description:
This provides a brief summary of the primary meaning of the few.

Word Oghams:
This lists the word oghams, or kennings, attributed to the few, followed by a commentary on the light these shed upon the few's original meaning.

Tree:
According to later tradition, each ogham was associated with a particular tree. This section suggests symbolic reasons for this association.

Deities and Heroes:
This section recounts those Celtic deities and heroic figures whose characters and exploits correspond most closely with the few.

Colour:
The symbolic colour associated with the few.

Bird:
Birds constitute another of the better-known oghamic word lists, and the symbolism is explored here.

Arts & Crafts / Profession:
The professional and artistic skills associated with the few are described.

Numerology:
The importance of the numeric sequence of the oghams cannot be stressed too highly.

Divinatory Meanings:
A full explanation of the influences suggested by the few in divination, complete with key words relating to its appearance in each of the fifths.

74

The Book of Ogham

```
>——┬
```

BEITHE – Birch-Tree
Vitality / Beginnings

Description:

Beithe is the first of the oghams, and it is therefore fitting that it should represent the idea of beginnings. It also represents life and vitality, since life – subjectively speaking – is the beginning. Beithe signifies enormous potential power for growth and development, it is bursting with energy. There is a great resonance between this few and the season of spring, when all of nature suddenly bursts into life and frenzied new growth after the barren winter.

Word Oghams:

Word Ogham of Morainn mac Moin: Withered foot with fine hair.
Word Ogham of Maic ind Oc: Greyest of skin.
Word Ogham of CúChulainn: Beauty of the eyebrow.

The name of the first ogham means 'birch-tree' and this is probably referred to in Maic ind Oc's phrase, 'greyest of skin', which is a good description of the silvery grey bark of the birch. Similarly, the smooth texture of this bark is not dissimilar to skin. This may be stretched to refer back to the association of the few with Otherworldly women, who were marked by their pale skin. This may also bring in the word of CúChulainn, 'beauty of the eyebrow', referring to the physical beauty of said women. Beauty is a secret key to open the ways to the Otherworld. What, specifically, is the beauty of an eyebrow? It is threefold: [1] its expressivity, in other words its capability to communicate the emotions, thoughts and intentions of its owner; [2] its shape, the curve which again suggests womanhood; [3] its hair. This latter leads us to Morainn mac Moin's word, 'withered foot with fine hair'. The kenning evidently refers to the birch, with its roots as the foot and its leaves as the hair, but let me stretch it a little and reread it as if it is the foot itself which has the hair. The notion of

75

hair on a foot being 'fine' or beautiful will puzzle most modern sensibilities, but in times past the sight of a woman's secret body hair was an incredibly erotic and intensely stimulating thing, a sensibility which will be lost on those who have been fooled by advertisers marketing shaving products. Fortunately, some few of us still recognise that nature knows best. The fact that the foot is withered refers of course to the shape of the roots of the birch tree, though it may have links to the fact that in some mythologies (such as the Aztec), a withered foot is often taken as a token of castration, which would again emphasise the female Mysteries of this particular few.

Tree:

The tree traditionally attributed to the B-few is the birch, a symbolically pleasing and appropriate tree for several reasons. As beithe is the first ogham, so birch is the first tree. It has been described as a "pioneer tree" and is usually the first species to appear on cleared land, growing at a much faster rate than other trees, as befits the vitality inherent in this few.

It has a silver/white bark which shines through its green foliage, which has always signified the Otherworld or Underworld in Celtic thought. This corresponds with the frequent image of the Otherworld woman, her white skin shining through slits in her green dress. Beithe was the first ogham to be written, seven times on a piece of birch to prevent abduction to the Otherworld. The symbolism of this few is very consistent.

Because of the intense vitality of the B-few, birch was long the favoured wood for judicial (or indeed recreational) floggings. The emphasis in using the birch is that its wholesome and stimulating vitality might prove a purgative to drive out evil or corrupt influence.

Deities and Heroes:

The goddess most closely associated with beithe is Brigid. This goddess, daughter of the Dagda, manifested a triple aspect as warrior, poet and mother: she is the mother, the giver of life; she is the warrior, who defends that life against anti-life forces; she is the poet, fulfilling the aesthetic function, giving that life meaning, shape and purpose.

Also linked to beithe is Badb, goddess of sovereignty, war and eroticism, who reappears in the later banshee ("Otherworld woman") legends. She champions the vitality, sovereignty and continuity of the house/family. Given the Celtic belief in rebirth through one's descendants the importance of this cannot be over-stressed.

Bran the mariner is also associated with beithe. He sailed with his crew on a voyage to the islands of the Otherworld. He returned close to the shores of Ireland and recorded his voyage to the Land of Women and the Island of Joy in ogham characters, then sailed away forever and was not heard from again. He signifies the pioneering spirit that is implicit within the B-few, the urge to always discover what lies over the crest of the next hill.

The figure of Bricriu is in some ways akin to certain aspects of the Norse God Loki, as he arranges a feast for kings and heroes, using it as an opportunity to set them against each other, inciting rivalries. This polarising, catalytic function often seems unwelcome when it manifests, but it is an essential process of bringing to the surface that which lies buried, for radical reappraisal. This too is part of the B-function, and it is in the hands of the individual whether this function proves to be a mire of contention or a catalyst for dynamic change.

Colour:

White is the colour most associated with beithe, signifying newness. This is the white page, which has not yet been written upon; it is the white light, which contains all of the other colours within it, just waiting to be loosed. It is a colour of new beginning and future potential.

Bird:

The pheasant is a bird very well attributed to the B-few, given its gregarious nature and the colourful plumage of the male. The fact that its young are born very well developed also resonates well with this ogham's emphasis upon vitality and beginnings. Young pheasants

77

The Book of Ogham

are capable of feeding themselves from birth, leave the nest within a few hours and can generally fly within a week.

Arts and Crafts / Profession:
    The profession associated with the B-few is that of the common labourer. It represents any task which is undertaken purely for the purpose of making a living, of sustaining life, for the ideal of this few is the propagation and sustenance of life itself. If this few arises in a divinatory context related to profession, it is probably referring to those tasks that you must do simply in order to maintain your life, prior to any secondary considerations.

Numerology:
    Beithe is numbered one, it is the first few of the first aicme. This requires little explanation: it is the beginning, the first manifestation. When all extraneous concerns and motivations are set aside and life is reduced to one thing, that thing is the essence of life itself and the potential beginning of all other things.

Divinatory Meanings:
    Beithe is concerned with births, with beginnings of things. It is possessed of an enormous vitality which can be channeled into new projects and aspirations. These influences can range from the literal birth of a new family member, the arrival of a new but significant person or influence in your life, a new job / career, a change for the better in terms of health (that surge of vital energy inherent in the few), or a complete change in lifestyle and circumstances.
    There is something intensely positive about beithe, and the changes and new beginnings with which it deals will almost always be positive too, a dynamic and fun adventure for those with the spirit to enjoy such things. But this does not imply that the process will always be painless. Even the good fortune of beithe has its price.
    Every change brings uncertainty, it involves the removal of the old and comfortable as well as the introduction of the new and exciting. Indeed, when beithe lands in a particularly fraught reading, its advice might imply the severance of old ties and patterns of life in

order to allow a chance for a fresh start. Although a positive step, this may also be a very painful and distressing one. It can involve loss and uncertainty, a lack of security for an indeterminate period of time.

The best way to approach the spirit of beithe is with an open mind and a sense of adventure, an intense curiosity about the larger world beyond your current horizons. Such an attitude will never fail to be rewarded by the current of beithe. Also, this few is tinged with the Otherworld – the image of the birch spoken of above, with the silver shining through the green. So keep an eye open for Otherworldly manifestations in relation to this few, such as strange synchronicities. These signs and omens become increasingly apparent when they are looked for by a prepared mind, and they can aid in anticipating the direction of, and best possible moment for, that new beginning.

The Fifths:

Beithe in Mide	Vitality in Sovereignty	Mead (+)
Beithe in Seis	Vitality in Harmony	Disturbance (-)
Beithe in Fis	Vitality in Learning	Eagerness (+)
Beithe in Cath	Vitality in Conflict	Fury (+)
Beithe in Blath	Vitality in Prosperity	Riches (+)

LUISE – Flame/Radiance, and LUS – Plant, Herb, Vegetable Insight / Quickening

Rowan

→ vitalizing

Description:

Luise concerns the development of insight and foreknowledge, and an awakening awareness of those influences which act upon you from outside of yourself so that these can be avoided,

79

controlled or modified. It is an increased objectivity, increased perception and increased self-reliance.

Luise operates upon the principle that once control is gained over one's perceptions and thoughts, then control is also gained over the other spheres of life. So much of what we do is manipulated by pre-programmed conditioning. In learning to see with a clear and focused perspective, so many new opportunities open before us, to which we were previously blind.

Word Oghams:
Word Ogham of Morainn mac Moin: Lustre of the eye.
Word Ogham of Maic ind Oc: Friend of cattle.
Word Ogham of CúChulainn: Sustenance of cattle.

The name of this ogham means 'flame' or 'radiance'. It is a name which the Irish later used to describe the rowan tree on account of the beauty of its berries, but the name does not in itself mean 'rowan'. This meaning implies the lively, quickening function of the few, something which is reflected in Morainn mac Moin's kenning, which applies this radiance to the eye, adding a dimension of consciousness. The other two kennings, 'friend of cattle' and 'sustenance of cattle' were, according to McManus, originally referred to the elm tree and were later transferred to the rowan. He comments, "cattle love the elm on account of its flower and its down". However, he also points out that these latter two kennings more likely refer to lus, meaning 'plant, herb, or vegetable' as an alternative name for the few.

Tree:
The tree later attributed to luise is the rowan, which favours high ground and when well placed is the most vibrant and brilliant of autumn colours, with leaves a brilliant orange. Its bright red berries display a similar liveliness. Perhaps it is this quality which gave it its alternate name of "quicken" tree, meaning "living wood".

As would be expected from a tree associated with the L-few and the quality of insight, the rowan has a long history of association with the practice of divination and magic. The druids spoke incantations over fires of rowan wood in order to invite the inhabitants of the sídhe to take part in battles. The tree is also said to provide protection from lightning and from malevolent enchantment.

Deities and Heroes:

Lugh Lamfadha is the god most closely corresponding to the L-few. He is the High God of the ancient Celts, and is named samildanach, "the many-skilled". Lugh boasts mastery of all the skills held by the other gods and thus is a king among them and a mighty magician. He is the chief warrior of the gods, wielder of a great spear. The straightness of the spear's shaft is symbolic of the will, directed with precision and passion, and the keenness of its point represents the clarity of perception inherent in luise. The war fought with this spear is against the forces of unconsciousness, it is a clear symbol of quickening, of lively intelligence. Lugh is probably the Celtic deity most closely corresponding to the Germanic Odin.

The Leanan Sidhe is an Otherworldly female figure said to live off the east coast of Ireland and haunt the Isle of Man at night. She inspires poets and musicians. In Manx lore, she is seen as a rather eerie figure who walks the land in the twilight hours and grants unearthly knowledge and "second sight" to those who earn her favour. She is therefore often feared, as people tend to fear the unknown.

In the heroic mythology, the L-few corresponds to Loegaire, the charioteer of CúChulainn, who travels to the Mag Mell to rescue its queen.

Colour:

The colour of luise is grey, a neutral shade that permits of no bias but fosters objectivity. It is the colour of the professional, of the dispassionate intellect.

Bird:

The duck is attributed to luise. This bird is a staple of country life, living in and by the waterways. Its colouring, environment and general robustness resonate well with this ogham.

81

The Book of Ogham

Arts and Crafts / Profession:

The skill associated with luise is that of the pilot or navigator, one who demonstrates insight on two levels, both equally important: firstly, he understands the purpose for the voyaging, where he is going and why; secondly, he has knowledge of the terrain he must pass through to get there, and is able to plot the most efficient course.

In contemporary life, a pilot or captain of a vessel would correspond with this few, but so would a "captain of industry" who guides the ship of the institution he manages.

Numerology:

Luise is the second of the oghams and thus represents duality. It emphasises the distinction between subject and object, observer and observed, etc. As such, it is a key to true objectivity of knowledge and perception.

Divinatory Meanings:

The L-few indicates that there exists within you a deep spring of insight and understanding that can be tapped to assist you in life. Its lesson is that no matter how bleak or negative your situation appears to be, the keys to its solution are to be found in the deep places of your own soul, if you can only reach for them.

Part of the key to this is a specific kind of detachment, the ability to forget your own involvement in and concerns with a situation, and see it as part of a larger picture, in its proper context. This objectivity can be of tremendous assistance in discovering where changes – whether in circumstances ot perspective – need to be made.

This insight is also useful in seeing the motivations of others clearly, and ensuring that you are not being manipulated or unduly influenced. This refers back to the use of rowan as a means of dispelling enchantments.

The shadow side of the L-few is that it can be very difficult to just set aside your worries and look at your situation through clear eyes. Sometimes the painful truth may be that the fault lies with your own actions or tendencies. It can also require a lot of courage sometimes to act upon your own inner conviction, contrary to the

The Book of Ogham

concerted opinion of those others around you.

The Fifths:

Luise in Mide	Insight in Sovereignty	Dominion (+)
Luise in Seis	Insight in Harmony	Craft (+)
Luise in Fis	Insight in Learning	Discovery (+)
Luise in Cath	Insight in Conflict	Cunning (+)
Luise in Blath	Insight in Prosperity	Abundance (+)

FERN – Alder-Tree
Foundation

Description:

The F-few refers to the "heart of the matter", the very roots of a situation. It stands for the founding principles and abiding truth, and thus is strongly linked to the past and remembrance.

As such, in the field of human activity it embodies such qualities as steadfastness and loyalty. This loyalty includes duty owed to others, but is equally a loyalty towards one's self and one's true principles.

Word Oghams:

Word Ogham of Morainn mac Moin: Vanguard of the warrior-band.
Word Ogham of Maic ind Oc: Container of milk.
Word Ogham of CúChulainn: Protection of the heart.

The ogham name means 'alder tree' and the kennings very obviously refer back to this meaning. The 'vanguard of the warrior-band' and 'protection of the heart' both refer to a shield – that which goes in front of the warrior and protects him – since shields were made of alder. Similarly, alder wood was used for milk pails. We might also draw some symbolic meaning from the function of the

The Book of Ogham

shield protecting the heart, which is the foundation of the body, and the warrior-band as the defender of the foundation of the community. Finally, the nourishment of milk is a foundation of life itself.

Tree:

Appropriately for a tree associated with the F-few and its foundational meaning, the alder has always been very highly prized for its timber. The tree is able to grow in wet and waterlogged conditions where others would perish through lack of nutrients in the soil, as its roots possess nodules which extract all that it needs from the air. Growing in such an environment made its timber enduring and resistant to rot and decay. A firm foundation indeed, as used at the Celtic lake dwellings at La Tène.

Because of this water resistant quality, the alder was believed to contain a fiery energy, representative of life force. Its white wood and red sap resembled the flesh and blood of a man which added to this symbolism. Both green and red dyes can be prepared from the alder (green from the leaves and red from the sap), leading to its association with the Otherworld and with life force and energy in general.

Deities and Heroes:

The god associated with fern is Fintan, who survived the primeval flood by dwelling underwater in a variety of shapes, most notably a salmon. Such an ancient being naturally became associated with an immense store of knowledge built up over the ages, and he represents the foundation of all true wisdom.

Fotla is one of the goddess forms representing the sovereignty of Ireland. As such, she represents the cultural and genetic foundation upon which life is built.

The hero best associated with fern is Finn mac Cumhail, around whom an entire heroic cycle of tales is woven. Finn was the great leader of the fianna warrior band in Ireland, and gained immense knowledge and magical power when he burnt his thumb whilst roasting the salmon of knowledge (see Fintan above) and put it in his mouth to cool it.

84

The Book of Ogham

Colour:

Fern's colour is red, representing the fiery energy that pervades the few. This fiery colour represents both the energy of self-sustained continuance, and the vigorous adherence to core principles.

Bird:

The gull is the bird attributed to the F-few. It has always symbolised great freedom, and nests along the coasts. Outside of the mating season, it is capable of living an entirely sea-bound existence. An old Celtic saying goes: "everything came from the sea, and everything will end with the sea."

Arts and Crafts / Profession:

The profession associated with the F-few is that of poet or bard. This goes far beyond the penning of verse as it is understood today, but encompasses a deep knowledge and appreciation of form, proportion, science and history.

The poetry of the bards was an operative magical process, which created change in the world around and in the listeners even as it was spoken. Deeper knowledge than the apparent surface meanings can be concealed in poetry by those who hold the keys - such as ogham attributions - to read it.

Numerology:

Fern is the third ogham, this representing the process of triangulation, of perceiving a situation from all sides and thus discerning its true essence. It emphasises the real over the apparent.

Divinatory Meanings:

The qualities contained within fern incorporate such aspects as steadfastness, integrity and objective knowledge. The few implies, or encourages, the discovery of underlying principles deep beneath the surface soap opera which surrounds any given situation. Fern goes directly to the root of a problem.

The F-few also emphasises the discovery of the founding principles within one's own self, the numinous apprehension of such questions as, "Who am I?", "What am I?", "Why am I?" The necessity of then reshaping one's whole life into an expression of these discovered principles goes without saying.

The danger in fern is the tendency to crystallise the founding principles discovered, to set them in stone, failing to realise that they – like life itself – can prosper only by evolving, a form of self-referential betterment as greater knowledge and wisdom becomes increasingly available. One's inner foundation is contextual to one's circumstances in life. As these change and greater life experience is won, so the very core of self experiences a maturation and a greater coming into being.

This is a vital point: fern is steadfastness, not stasis.

The Fifths:

Fern in Mide	Foundation in Sovereignty	Principles (+)
Fern in Seis	Foundation in Harmony	Quickness (+)
Fern in Fis	Foundation in Learning	Laziness (-)
Fern in Cath	Foundation in Conflict	Vigilance (+)
Fern in Blath	Foundation in Prosperity	Obstruction (-)

SAIL - Willow-Tree
Intuition

Description:

The S-few refers to the intuitive faculties, including psychic abilities, clairvoyance and imagination. It is linked to all things watery and lunar.

The few embodies all of those impulses and insights that arise in the normally subconscious parts of the psyche.

Word Oghams:

Word Ogham of Morainn mac Moin: Pallor of a dead man.

86

The Book of Ogham

Word Ogham of Mac ind Oc: Sustenance of bees.
Word Ogham of CúChulainn: Beginning of honey.

    The name refers to the willow tree, often called the sally-tree to this day. The 'pallor of a dead man' is evidently a reference to the colour of the tree. It also reminds us of the Underworld, pertinent given the few's association with water and the subconscious. 'Sustenance of bees' and 'beginning of honey' point to the catkins of the willow, the pollen of which is taken by the bees to produce honey. The whole process of producing honey is taken as a metaphor for the acquisition of wisdom and thus resonates with the few's meaning of intuition and developing insight.

Tree:

    The tree attributed to sail is one long linked with water and dreamy intuition, namely the willow. It has a great affinity with watery places and its magical symbolism is quite superbly captured in the character of "Old Man Willow" in the "Old Forest" section of J.R.R. Tolkien's novel, The Lord of the Rings.

    Branches of the willow are often used to supplement human intuitive faculties through their use as divining rods, and the willow was one of the three woods used in the fabrication of the traditional witch's broom, willow being used to bind birch twigs to an ash stake.

Deities and Heroes:

    The deity associated with sail is Semias, the master of wisdom who dwells in the west in the Otherworld city of Murias. Semias was the original possessor of the cauldron of knowledge, a magnificent symbol for the S-few. He gave the cauldron to the Dagda.

    Among the goddesses, the few is associated with Scathach, who teaches CúChulainn skill with arms, but also exercises the S-related function of foretelling his future.

    Among the heroes, Setanta was the boyhood name of CúChulainn, representing the potential that lay within him but was still dormant (unconscious) at that point in his development.

The Book of Ogham

Colour:

The colour ascribed to the S-few translates as "fine-coloured". So the exact tint would not seem to be vitally important – the subconscious holds many hues – but the subtlety of the shade is to be emphasised.

Bird:

The hawk is attributed to sail, a bird of prey. The expression "the eyes of a hawk" has passed down to us today, and emphasises the ability to discern and perceive that which others do not see.

Arts and Crafts / Profession:

The skill associated with the S-few is that of handicrafts, i.e. those tasks or crafts which rely upon a certain skill to make or shape something. This is the process of using learned skills or natural talents to shape in physical form those things seen in the mind's eye.

Numerology:

Sail is the fourth ogham, and this number refers to the division of the natural order into four quarters, the four directions. As with the four seasons, this is a number which speaks of the completion of cycles in the natural world. This resonates with the ability of the psyche to recognise and read the patterns of these cycles in an intuitive or divinatory manner.

Divinatory Meanings:

Sail deals with undercurrents, with those things which pass beneath the surface of observable everyday life, but which nonetheless influence its course. As such, its concern is with unforeseen dangers or unexpected events. In a divinatory context, the few warns against factors which have not been recognised or taken into account by the querent. It engages the intuitive faculties to gain greater cognisance of these factors, or indeed to influence or reshape them in some way.

Sail refers to the powers of the imagination. It promotes the development of psychic abilities and can be used to enhance the recall of dreams, or dream work in general.

The Book of Ogham

The danger of this few is one of proper psychic balance, in that the imagination can be accorded too much significance, leading to delusion or lunacy (the very name, derived from luna - the moon - makes plain the danger.) On the other hand, there is an equal and opposite danger of ignoring the intuition altogether and rationalising everything away, leading to a hollow and empty existence.

The Fifths:

Sail in Mide	Intuition in Sovereignty	Insight (+)
Sail in Seis	Intuition in Harmony	Subtlety (+)
Sail in Fis	Intuition in Learning	Cunning (+)
Sail in Cath	Intuition in Conflict	Advantage (+)
Sail in Blath	Intuition in Prosperity	Loathing (-)

NIN - Forked Branch / Lofty Rebirth / Peace

Description:
　　Nin represents the link and interplay between the inner and outer worlds. It is the mesh of cause and effect, but also takes into account causes which may be hidden and thus might seem acausal to the untrained eye. It is the ending and beginning of cycles of becoming.

　　The few promotes the cultivation of a large scale view of the universe, and assists in always seeing the bigger picture. Those who grasp the inner meaning of nin are able to discern the factors which determine the ways in which reality takes shape and manifests itself. It assists in harmonising inner vision with outer happening.

Word Oghams:
Word Ogham of Morainn mac Moin: Establishing of peace.

The Book of Ogham

Word Ogham of Maic ind Oc: Boast of women.
Word Ogham of CúChulainn: Boast of beauty.

      The first kenning, 'beginning of peace' refers in a roundabout way to the ash tree which became associated with this few. Nin is the fork of a weaver's beam, which was only erected in times of peace, being made of ash, which would otherwise be used to make spears. 'Boast of women' and 'boast of beauty' both carry the same implication, since the weaver's beam would be used to craft fine garments to beautify the wearer. The whole expresses the meaning of nin: the establishment of peace and new beginnings through the application of resources to items of beauty instead of war. If I was to be facetious (and I usually am, so why stop now?), I would point out that the word nin can mean 'the letter n and letters in general', bringing to mind our modern saying that the pen is mightier than the sword. This would be a wholly appropriate interpretation of the few, and it is an interesting and entertaining coincidence that a modern saying should echo its meaning so clearly. The meaning of 'forked branch' refers perhaps to the shaking of the olive branch in Irish tradition, at which men would stop fighting. This would accord with the 'beginning of peace' kenning and the few's generally accepted meaning.

Tree:

      In later times the ash tree was attributed to the N-few, and the cosmological symbolism of the few is expressed in the tree's compound leaves: these generally form the pattern of one single leaflet together with two or four pairs of leaflets. The total number of leaflets in each compound leaf therefore totals either five or nine, which have already been established as numbers of cosmic significance to the Celts.

      The wood of the ash was often used in the fabrication of spears.

Deities and Heroes:

      The god associated with the N-few is Nuada Airgetlam (Silver Arm). Nuada was king of the Tuatha Dé Danann and lost his hand in battle. He had a replacement made of silver, but passed the kingship to Lugh, since the king had to be unblemished in body. He later resumed the kingship when a new flesh hand was grafted on and then he was slain in the battle of Mag Tured. The importance of both honour and perfection in the kingly man are expressed in this tale. The similarity to the Germanic Tyr is obvious.

Also linked with this few is Nodens, a Celtic god of the waters.

Niamh, the daughter of Manannán, another deity related to the sea, is the goddess associated with nin. She lured Oisin into Tír na n'Og for three hundred years, showing the few's aspects of peace and the connections between worlds.

The hero associated with N is Niall. He too, like Nuada, became a king, and he too is linked with water. He attained the crown by obtaining water from a hag, and in order to do this he first had to lie with her. Afterwards, the hag – or Caillach – revealed herself to be the goddess Ériu, a Form of the Sovereignty of Ireland. This tale demonstrates the power inherent within the few to see beyond the surface appearance of things into their true underlying principles.

Colour:

The colour attributed to nin is necht, "clear". This refers to transparency, to the ability to discern the true meaning and significance of an event or situation in all worlds.

Bird:

The snipe is attributed to nin. It is a wader bird, foraging mainly at dawn and dusk, the "crossover" or "in-between" times of the day.

Arts and Crafts / Profession:

The profession linked to the N-few is notary work, or accountancy. This type of work involves a full objective assessment and statement of the true worth and well-being of a corporation or individual. It requires a meticulous eye and an appreciation of the whole scope of the organisation.

The Book of Ogham

Numerology:

N is the fifth ogham few, and the final few in the first group. In Celtic cosmology, the number five was representative of the universe: the four directions and the centre, as in the division of Ireland. This sense of completion and an all-encompassing influence accords well with the few's meaning.

Divinatory Meanings:

Nin represents the perfected model of Celtic cosmological wisdom, as the five expands into the multi-dimensional model of the various worlds (see chapter 2). As such, it represents true visionary abilities, always seeing the larger picture and discerning the truth behind surface appearances.

The cosmic balance of this few is indicative of its twin meanings: peace and rebirth. At first glance, these two appear contradictory, as peace is a passive state of being, whereas rebirth is intensely active. In truth, they are the two poles of a single process, harmonised in nin. The fivefold patterning of the few signifies the end of one cycle of being and the commencement of another. As the peak of one cycle is reached and a new perspective is attained, a sense of peace is prevalent, a time of respite and integration of all that has been learned. The wheel continues to turn, however, launching into a new process of activity, albeit from a loftier starting point; it is an ascending spiral rather than a return to the exact same place.

The Fifths:

Nin in Mide	Rebirth in Sovereignty	Renewal (+)
Nin in Seis	Rebirth in Harmony	Tyranny (-)
Nin in Fis	Rebirth in Learning	Satisfaction (+)
Nin in Cath	Rebirth in Conflict	Affluence (+)
Nin in Blath	Rebirth in Prosperity	Impoverishment (-)

The Book of Ogham

>—⊥

hUATH – Fear, Horror
Misfortune

Description:

 Uath is a grim few, with an emphasis upon negative influences within life. It governs misfortune and bad luck in general. When everything that can go wrong does go wrong, depression sets in and life seems dismal, that's the influence of úath.

 The few also has a more mysterious side which encourages spiritual growth for those able to perceive it, but in terms of everyday life this is a miserable portent.

Word Oghams:
Word Ogham of Morainn mac Moin: Assembly of packs of hounds.
Word Ogham of Maic ind Oc: Blanching of faces.
Word Ogham of CúChulainn: Most difficult at night.

 This few is linked with misfortune, its name meaning 'fear' or 'horror'. 'Assembly of packs of hounds' refers to the terror felt by a person confronted by a wolf pack. The wolves are also symbolic of the fearful thorns of the whitethorn, though this is a later association. 'Blanching of faces' is a self-evident kenning for the effect of fear on a person and fear is 'most difficult at night', when one is forced to deal with it alone in the dark. McManus postulates that the few's name is derived from the root *au-, meaning 'down, away from', which would suggest an Underworld connection.

Tree:

 The hawthorn was the tree later attributed to the H-few. It has long been a sacred tree in the British Isles and is strongly linked to the Beltaine festival and the May Day revelries. Before the Gregorian Calendar was introduced to Britain in 1752, effectively moving the old May 1st to the new May 13th, May Day had been the usual date of full

93

The Book of Ogham

flowering for the hawthorn, marking this important turn in the year.

The hawthorn partakes of the rather ambivalent nature of this time of transition, which is neither one season nor the other. In particular, it has a dual sexual significance – often echoed in the old May day revels – and symbolises both sexual abandon and sexual abstinence.

Deities and Heroes:

The intrinsic malevolence and ill-fortune of the H-few is amply illustrated by the fact that there are no gods or heroes among the Celts whose names begin with this letter.

This does, however, hint at a secret, hidden aspect to the few, concealed from the eyes of the profane.

In terms of recognising the manifestation of the úath-principle in the world, it is associated with those things which may have a beautiful, alluring and seductive outer appearance, but are deadly and harmful underneath their surface glamour.

Colour:

The colour ascribed to úath is "terrible". In other words, it is any shade which is glaring, threatening or ominous, shades that the mind associates with harm or impending doom.

Bird:

The night raven is the bird attributed to the H-few. These large, black, raucous birds have long been considered creatures of ill omen, presaging death or other misfortune. As Marlowe eloquently put it, "The sad presaging raven tolls the sick man's passport in her beak."

Arts and Crafts / Profession:

The craft attributed to úath is that of trisyllabic poetry. This is a hint at one aspect of the higher mystery of this few.

Numerology:

The number of úath is six. In the Celtic paradigm, five is the

94

number of completion (with nine as its harmonic). Six therefore represents a new beginning following the ending of a cycle. (This is clearly implied in the meaning of nin, the previous ogham, and in úath's position as the first in the second group of five fews.) However, nothing is so difficult as starting out again. Once that final position of equilibrium and satisfaction is achieved at the close of one cycle of being, the forces of inertia (including internal ones, such as the feeling of satisfaction at a "job well done") strive to maintain that position and inhibit further motion. This is why it is so difficult and painful to start a fresh process of becoming, and so easy to slip into comfortable stasis. Continued progress is hard, and úath reflects this; it is the increasing strain and tension between striving to remain in the prior state while the wheel increasingly pulls forward.

Divinatory Meanings:

The H-few generally implies disruption in the ordinary affairs of life. It may involve a streak of bad luck, it may involve intentional malice against you from some source. The message underlying these symptoms is generally the same: step back, take stock of your life, identify what is necessary, then move on.

This misfortune may come from within as well as from without. You may be secretly sabotaging yourself because you inwardly realise that you are making no headway and that it is time for a change, a re-evaluation of your life. In such a case, the best course of action is to stop, take time out to think, set your life in order. Then, and only then, is the time to move on. Similarly, if somebody else is deliberately causing trouble for you, don't just charge in with a battle standard raised. First take time to reflect: is this perhaps your fault? Is there something you have or haven't done to provoke this person, and can it be set right? If not, then gather your objective facts as ammunition before tackling anything head on.

The unpleasantness associated with úath is always a warning that it is time to pause and check the direction and purpose of your life.

The Book of Ogham

Uath in Mide	Misfortune in Sovereignty	Weakness (-)
Uath in Seis	Misfortune in Harmony	Disharmony (-)
Uath in Fis	Misfortune in Learning	Ignorance (-)
Uath in Cath	Misfortune in Conflict	Defeat (-)
Uath in Blath	Misfortune in Prosperity	Poverty (-)

DUIR – Oak-tree
Endurance

Description:

Duir is indicative of such qualities as stamina, strength and endurance. It is the sheer determination and drive to overcome any challenge and succeed at any test, no matter how poor the odds.

Although it does cover the aspect of physical strength and endurance, its primary emphasis is upon strength of character and will, of steely determination and the adherence to principles of steadfastness, loyalty, truth and courage.

Word Oghams:

Word Ogham of Morainn mac Moin: Most exalted tree.

Word Ogham of Maic ind Oc: Handicraft of an artificer.

Word Ogham of CúChulainn: Most carved of craftsmanship.

'Oak tree' is the meaning of the few and the kennings obviously refer directly back to this. Oak has long been known to be the tree viewed as 'most exalted' by the druids. The other two word oghams refer to its use in woodwork and craftsmanship, a sturdy and durable wood of supreme usefulness.

Tree:

The oak is attributed to the D-few, and as befits this ogham it is one of the most robust of trees, with very deep roots. It rarely suffers, even in drought. Its name has to do with hardness and steadfastness, being derived from the Indo-European root *deru-, to be firm, steadfast. This is the root which gives us not only "tree" in English, but also "truth" and "troth". One etymology of the word "druid" derives it from *dru-wid, "knower of oak trees" -- although it could just as easily mean "knower of the truth or troth", i.e. "steadfast knowledge".

The oak was certainly greatly revered by the druids, and oak groves were probably the typical sites for nemetons throughout the Celtic world. Their environs are considered especially auspicious for workings of magic or divination, and it was thought that the druid could gain special insight and wisdom by eating acorns.

Oaks invariably grow to a great size and live to a great age: Arthur's round table at Winchester is cut from a single slice of an enormous oak tree.

Deities and Heroes:

The god associated with the D-few is the Dagda, the "good god". This title is not necessarily a statement of moral character, but rather implies that this god is good, i.e. skilled and praiseworthy, at everything he turns his hands to. The Dagda was in all likelihood originally the chief god of the Irish, a Celtic version of a Zeus figure. His weapon was a tremendous club, and he was the god most revered by the druids (with whom he is strongly associated through the duir ogham). The Dagda has a cauldron which dispenses never-ending blessings, and it is this cauldron which receives the sacrifices of the druids. The Dagda also possesses a magical harp called "the Oak of Two Greens" and "the four-angled music", with which he plays three spells woven into his music: the laugh-strain, the sorrow-strain and the sleep-strain. The Dagda is one of the most ancient figures in Celtic religion and is the father of Brigid.

The goddess Danu also stresses the ancient roots of Celtic religion, as she is the oldest and most remote ancestress of the gods, who are named the Tuatha Dé Danann (the people of Danu) after her.

The Book of Ogham

In the heroic tales, there are two figures who exemplify the qualities of the D-few. Both are tragic heroes in the true literary sense, figures who – although they are finally overcome by overwhelming odds – nevertheless display great steadfastness and endurance in the process.

The first of these is Deirdriu, who was secretly fostered as a child after the druid Cathbad prophesied that when fully grown she would bring destruction to Ulster. Sure enough, she was so fair that many men desired her and the resulting wars over her ravaged the province. Finally, to prevent further conflict, she killed herself. There is a strong resemblance between her tale and that of Helen of Troy.

Another hero was Diarmuid, a nephew of Finn who was brought up in the Underworld and possessed a love spot which made him irresistible to women. He accompanies the aging Finn, who seeks to acquire a young wife named Grainne. However, the maiden falls in love with Diarmuid and the pair elope. They are pursued by the enraged Finn, who lays a geis upon them that they may not spend more than one night in any place. Eventually, Finn and Diarmuid make their peace, but Finn leads Diarmuid on a boar hunt, violating a geis. Diarmuid is fatally wounded and Finn's jealousy rises within him again. The hands of Finn are healing, but he delays too long in bringing the healing drink to Diarmuid, who dies. This tale can be compared to that of Tristan and Isolde in the Celtic Arthurian myths.

Colour:

The colour of duir is black, as it is a very heavy and "solid" colour, one which absorbs other colours into itself. Black is also the most ancient colour, predating even the light. It is a solemn colour, as the D-few stresses duty, loyalty and truth.

Bird:

The wren is the bird attributed to duir. This accords with the few's stable and enduring emphasis, for the wren builds elaborate roofed nests, which are used not only to house eggs, but also as communal roosts.

98

The Book of Ogham

Arts and Crafts / Profession:

The oak and its few are associated with the practice of wizardry, with the Celtic druids. Great in knowledge, deep in wisdom, with the roots of their religion in the ancient past.

The carpenter is also associated with the D-few, the painstaking creation of works of aesthetic or utilitarian integrity from the living wood. "Integrity" is a good word to describe all aspects of duir.

Numerology:

Duir is the seventh ogham few. In general numerology, seven is considered to be a sacred or divine number, and this accords well with the nature of the few.

In the order of oghams, duir is the second few of the second fifth. It therefore restates the principle of duality. It stresses poles and those extremes and opposites which meet in the few, balanced and reconciled by the principle of truth

Divinatory Meanings:

The primary meaning of duir is one of strength, courage and endurance. It is the courage to be true to one's most fundamental principles in the face of all opposition, to stand as steadfast and proud as an old oak in the face of the storm. There is a deep honour and heroism about the few.

Great knowledge and wisdom is also associated with duir, as befits its strong links with the druids. There is a sense of great age about this few, and those who can apprehend its essence can gaze both backwards and forwards through the mists of time to discern the patterns of unfolding events. Duir is a boundary between realms, between the past and the future, as well as between this world, the Underworld and the Otherworld.

The main thrust of this few in most situations is to be sure of your principles, stick to your guns, and lead instead of following. There is a difference between steadfastness and obstinacy, however, and confusing the two is the chief danger of the D-few.

The Book of Ogham

The Fifths:

Duir in Mide	Endurance in Sovereignty	Realisation (+)
Duir in Seis	Endurance in Harmony	Discontent (-)
Duir in Fis	Endurance in Learning	Recognition (+)
Duir in Cath	Endurance in Conflict	Destruction (+)
Duir in Blath	Endurance in Prosperity	Rest (+)

TINNE – Bar, Rod of Metal, Ingot, Mass of Molten Metal
Balance

Description:

Tinne represents the force of balance as actively applied in life. As such, it encompasses such ideas as justice for wrongs done, reward for good deeds, etc.

This is not necessarily a moral balance, it can imply simple exchanges of tit for tat. As such, the responsibility for judging the right or wrong of a situation remains very much with the individual considering taking action.

Tinne brings with it the recognition that the deeds of the past shape the present, and the present must be interpreted in the light of those deeds.

Word Oghams:

Word Ogham of Morainn mac Moin: One of three parts of a wheel.

Word Ogham of Maic ind Oc: Marrow of coal.

Word Ogham of CúChulainn: One of three parts of a weapon.

The first kenning refers to the wood of the holly tree to which the few was later attributed. Holly is one of the three kinds of wood used to make a chariot wheel. The final kenning, 'one of three

100

parts of a weapon' refers to the few's original meaning, namely iron. Maic ind Oc's phrase is a reference to the smelting process. Tinne's divinatory / magical meaning of 'balance' is perhaps suggested by the fact that two of its word oghams identify it as 'one of three parts' of some item and that it is the third ogham in its row, with three strokes to mark it. In all of these cases, the number three suggests two ends and a middle, which is the balancing point between them. Tinne is all about precision.

Tree:

Later in the Middle Ages the holly was associated with the T-few, an evergreen tree which grows spiky leaves, emphasising the actively defensive nature of the ogham.

The wood of the holly used to be used in the construction of chariot shafts, and in the tale of Sir Gawain and the Green Knight, the Green Knight – indicated as a supernatural warrior of the Otherworld by his colour – used a great club of holly.

The tree's evergreen leaves and brilliant red berries which shine out in the bleakness of winter are still displayed in homes at the time of the winter solstice, to bring their vitality into the homestead. Very often, the red berries of the holly survive right through the winter until May.

Deities and Heroes:

The god associated with tinne is Trefuilngid Tre-Eochair, a primordial entity who instructed the men of Ireland in the division of the land according to the fivefold cosmological structure, a patterning and balancing of the kingdom after the proper ordering of the Celtic cosmos. He was also described as controlling the rising and the setting of the sun, thus the proper balancing and regulation of time.

The hero of this few is Tigernmas, the individual said to have introduced the cult of Cromm Cruach. He also introduced metallurgy and the weaving of tartans as clan insignia. This latter is particularly interesting in the light of this few, as the clan tartan provides an immediately observable statement of ancestral heritage and clan relations, crucial to the proper ordering of society. His connection with metallurgy requires no further elaboration given the original name and symbolism of the T-few.

Colour:

The colour attributed to tinne is dark grey, a stern but neutral colour, which speaks of the laws and orderings which bind beings to the cosmic processes. It is the weight of obligation, which is at one and the same time both oppressive and liberating.

Bird:

The starling is attributed to the T-few. This bird came to be well-regarded as a natural balancing factor by European farmers many centuries ago, due to its efficiency in destroying the insect populations which threatened the crops.

Arts and Crafts / Profession:

The profession attributed to tinne is that of the turner, i.e. one who makes wheels and axles for chariots – as well as the iron rim that went around the best of them. In contemporary terms, this could apply to any mechanical or engineering skill. The emphasis is upon precision work which produces a well balanced, properly proportioned, smooth running end product.

Numerology:

The number of the T-few is eight, a number of solidity and stability. It is the eight spokes of a cosmic wheel (the ninth point being the centre), which accords well with the balancing nature of the few.

Divinatory Meanings:

At its best, tinne is indicative of a directed balance, the ability to weigh all sides of a question and decide upon a proportionate response which will best further one's goals in the light of the circumstances. It also signifies justice and retribution for wrong-doing, and carries a sense of honour and duty.

The T- and D-sounds are linked, the only difference between their pronunciation being that when making the D-sound the

The Book of Ogham

vocal chords vibrate, whereas they do not for the T-sound (much of bardic magic revolves around these patterns of sounds, be closely heedful of them). It is through the measured actions of tinne that the principles and troth of duir are defended and upheld.

The negative aspect of the T-few occurs when balance becomes rigid, and instead of providing a pattern for life, in which evolution and progression may occur, it instead becomes a form of bondage to the status quo, an inertial trap which resists all change. There is thus a need for a healthy antinomianism when dealing with tinne, a recognition that sometimes rules were made to be broken and are not the be-all and end-all in their own right; they were framed to serve a purpose, whose circumstances can alter. This too is a form of balance.

The Fifths:

Tinne in Mide	Balance in Sovereignty	Steadfastness (+)
Tinne in Seis	Balance in Harmony	Rejection (-)
Tinne in Fis	Balance in Learning	Judgement (+)
Tinne in Cath	Balance in Conflict	Vengeance (+)
Tinne in Blath	Balance in Prosperity	Preparation (+)

COLL – Hazel
Creativity

Description:

Coll represents the innate creativity of the human spirit, that spark of genius which is something much more than the biological machine in which it resides. It is the deep well of inspiration that lies in the hidden places of the soul, and it is the means by which communication occurs between this creative impulse and the outside world – a communication in both directions.

The Book of Ogham

Word Oghams:
Word Ogham of Morainn mac Moin: Fairest tree.
Word Ogham of Maic ind Oc: Friend of nutshells.
Word Ogham of CúChulainn: Sweetest tree.

All of the kennings refer to the hazel tree or to its nuts (that of Maic ind Oc referencing the empty shells since everyone eats the nuts because they are so appealing). The emphasis upon fairness and sweetness is highly appropriate to the few's creative leanings and the allusions to eating the nuts refers back to the mythic hazel in the Underworld, whose nuts fall into the stream to be eaten by the salmon: all symbols of hidden knowledge and creative thought.

Tree:

The hazel, a tree which first appeared in Britain in the wake of the Ice Age, is attributed to the C-few.

The most striking myth featuring the hazel is that of Cormac, who traveled to the Otherworld to try to recover his wife, son and daughter, who had been abducted by Manannán mac Lir. While there, he saw a spring with nine hazels growing over it. The nuts of the nine hazels fall into the water, making the sweetest music ever heard. The nuts are then eaten by the five salmon who live in the pool, who seperate the fruit of the nuts from their shells and send the shells down the five streams which lead off from the pool. Eventually it is revealed to Cormac that this is the Spring of Knowledge, out of which flow the streams of the five senses, through which knowledge is obtained. Manannán says that to become one of the "people of may arts", one must drink directly from the spring as well as from the streams.

Deities and Heroes:

The god attributed to the C-few is the primeval being known as Cian mac Cainte, the father of Lugh, i.e. the source from which the magician-king issued.

The goddess is the Caillach, the divine hag who rules the year from Samhain to Beltaine. She represents the deep wells of feminine mysteries, including those which are generally unspoken for their dark and sinister nature.

CúChulainn is the hero of this few, probably the fieriest and most colourful of the Irish heroes. His myths are numerous and can be found in the Ulster Cycle of tales. He represents the manifestation of the will through flesh and blood.

Cormac also resonates with this few, as described in the tree correspondence above.

Colour:

Brown is the colour of this ogham, representing the rich and fertile earth, from which new life and creation arises.

Bird:

In the traditional lists in the manuscripts, no bird attribution is generally given for the C-few, but I would suggest the cuckoo (Manx Gaelic cooag) as a suitable choice, for the creative manner in which it ensures the survival and nurturing of its young.

Arts and Crafts / Profession:

The profession associated with the few is that of harpist or musician. This is the creative skill which renders tangible the insights afforded by the few, and expresses that creativity in ways which can be communicated to others in music. In this regard, the great importance of music to the Celts should be remembered, along with the magical powers they attributed to it.

Numerology:

Coll is numbered nine, another number of cosmological significance to the Celts. The basic cosmic pattern is fivefold - four quarters and a centre - but this becomes nine when the quarters are extended beyond themselves into other dimensions. This ninefold pattern was a fairly common scheme given the high incidence of interdimensionality in the Celtic mindset. The cosmological map in chapter 2 reveals this world (bith), together with four Otherworld realms and four Underworld realms, for nine worlds in total.

The Book of Ogham

Divinatory Meanings:

Coll represents the entire creative impulse and the ability to work with it and express it. As such, it has three aspects:

1. The ability to see beyond the mere outer shape of a thing or an idea, perceiving its innermost essence, those rarefied qualities which truly make it what it is. This is the aspect of recognition.

2. The ability to perceive new and wonderful ways in which these qualities may be expressed and manipulated. This is the aspect of creativity.

3. The application of due skill and mastery in your craft to express these essential qualities in ways in which they can be appreciated by other people, and can move them in the way you intended. This is the aspect of work.

All three aspects are essential to appreciate and gainfully use the process of this ogham. Everybody possesses all three qualities in their unique measure. Failure most often occurs when vain people exercise the wrong craft in order to fit in with their peer group, instead of that to which they are most suited. Find your own creative outlets and use them.

Through exercise of the qualities of this few, you can learn to apply its principles in all of life's situations, and can bring creative and inspiring solutions to bear upon many human problems, simply by mixing the essential qualities of the situation in new and refreshing ways. Ultimately, life becomes a wonderful and stimulating game.

The Fifths:

Coll in Mide	Creativity in Sovereignty	Eloquence (+)
Coll in Seis	Creativity in Harmony	Beauty (+)
Coll in Fis	Creativity in Learning	Teaching (+)
Coll in Cath	Creativity in Conflict	Arbitration (+)
Coll in Blath	Creativity in Prosperity	Arts (+)

The Book of Ogham

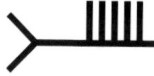

>IIIII

CERT – Bush / Rag
Beauty / Eternity

Description:

The Q-few represents all that is beautiful, embodying the principles of proportion and harmony. Linked to this is the idea of eternity, as that which is truly beautiful must be beautiful eternally. It therefore resonates strongly with the Celtic ideals of youth and vitality.

These principles are applied on a grand scale, however. There is something cosmic and vast about this few.

Word Oghams:

Word Ogham of Morainn mac Moin: Shelter of a lunatic.
Word Ogham of Maic ind Oc: Substance of an insignificant person.
Word Ogham of CúChulainn: Dregs of clothing.

All three kennings refer quite plainly to rags. The lunatic and the 'insignificant person' are both clad in rags and this is made explicit by the third, 'dregs of clothing'. This may seem strange for a few whose meaning is beauty, but quite the contrary is true. The few's other meaning is eternity and the beauty it speaks of is eternal, not to be found in gaudy clothing. It is a beauty as much of the mind, and the lunatic is peculiarly associated with this ogham. There is an alternate reading / interpretation of the word ogham of Morainn mac Moin, which suggests the meaning of 'bush' (the meaning may be 'shelter of a lunatic' or 'shelter of a hind / doe', which suggests bushes and woodlands) and it is from this that the later association with the apple was probably derived.

Tree:

The tree which later associated with the Q-few is the apple tree. The apple is a sweet and healthy fruit, and its use to make the alcoholic drink cider gives it links to the Underworld.

The Book of Ogham

The fivefold arrangement of the apple's seeds brings to mind the mysteries of the pentagram, which conceals within its design the key to proportionate beauty in the phi ratio, or "golden ratio".

In Irish myth, Manannán mac Lir possessed a silver branch, from which hung three golden apples. This branch, called the craebh ciuil, made sweet music which inspired joy. It had the power to heal the sick, and could cause people to go to sleep if it was shaken towards them.

Deities and Heroes:
In Gaelic tongues, the sound of the letter Q is interchangeable with the of the letter C. The letter does have a subtle meaning of its own, however, and is by no means redundant. It occurs with astonishing regularity at the head of Manx surnames (Quayle, Quiggin, Quane, Quine, Quirk, Qualtrough, etc.)

Those deities and heroes attributed to coll might also be considered to have an affinity with cert. However, due to the latter's cosmic significance, there is also the hint of a Hidden God or Hero who is in slumber, awaiting the moment of awakening. The archetypal image of the this figure might be similar to Arthur or Merlin, who sleep awaiting their return to the lands of mortals. In some ways the mystery of this hidden figure is individual to each seeker and must be sought on that basis.

Colour:
The colour attributed to this few -- "mouse coloured" -- may seem strange at first when considering the surface meaning of cert. Probe a little deeper into the few's meaning, however, and it starts to seem more appropriate. The colour of a mouse blends it unobtrusively in with its surroundings, allowing it to go about its quiet business undisturbed by the larger creatures of the house. This resonates with the harmonious but also subtle and secret meanings of this ogham.

Bird:
The hen is attributed to the Q-few. This is probably due to

108

The Book of Ogham

its domestication and value to man over the centuries.

Arts and Crafts / Profession:

The profession attributed to cert is that of the flute player. The beautiful and haunting notes of the flute accord very well indeed with the ogham; it is an instrument supremely capable of evoking a sense of beauty. The flute is not without magical lore of its own, and its subtler notes may penetrate many words and realms beyond the merely physical. Beauty is more than skin deep, as the saying goes.

Numerology:

The number of cert is ten, which speaks of completion and perfection, but also of new beginnings. The number ten represents a return to beginnings, the decimal scale has moved full circle. But this beginning is at a higher level than the one before. This hints at both the perfection implied in this ogham, and also at the cyclical nature of eternity.

The number five is also especially associated with cert, as it is the fifth few of the second aicme. As mentioned in the section on the apple tree attribution above, the mystery of the Pythagorean pentagram and the phi ratio is linked with this few; the supposition that the proportions which define that which is beautiful are not arbitrary.

Divinatory Meanings:

The primary meaning of cert is to seek after beauty and proportion in all things. The thrust of this idea is something a little strange to modern minds, where beauty is perceived as something passive to be admired, instead of something active to be aspired towards.

This is perhaps made clearer when considering the ogham's links with eternity. In his Symposium, Plato made a strong argument for a link between the principles of beauty and eternity. True beauty, in order to be fully beautiful, must also by definition be immortal, otherwise its beauty is spoiled. Seeking after beauty therefore transmutes into the quest for immortality.

The Book of Ogham

This is where cert becomes slightly more sinister for those who are unprepared for it, just as cider quickly unbalances the brain unaccustomed to such a sweet drink being so potently alcoholic. Cert incorporates an understanding of vast cycles of time, incorporating one's own death and potential after-death state. This should be no surprise for a few with such strong connections with the Underworld.

Another danger of cert is that beauty is addictive and distracting for the undisciplined mind. The lesson is that it is all too easy to be dazzled and mesmerised by surface glamours instead of looking for the deeper principles.

The Fifths:

Cert in Mide	Eternity in Sovereignty	Perfection (+)
Cert in Seis	Eternity in Harmony	Satisfaction (+)
Cert in Fis	Eternity in Learning	Esoterica (+)
Cert in Cath	Eternity in Conflict	Doubt (-)
Cert in Blath	Eternity in Prosperity	Completion (+)

MUIN – Neck / Trick / Love
Inwardness

Description:

The M-few represents the interweaving of the inner and outer worlds, the subjective and objective experiences of reality. On a personal level, it is the touching and intertwining of the conscious and subconscious strata of the psyche. On a transpersonal level, it is the awareness of Self and Not-Self and the influence that each has upon the other.

The most potent meaning of muin is that of making inner knowledge and vision manifest in outer, objective reality. It is the transition from dream to waking, and vice versa.

The Book of Ogham

Word Oghams:
Word Ogham of Morainn mac Moin: Strongest in exertion.
Word Ogham of Maic ind Oc: Proverb of slaughter.
Word Ogham of CúChulainn: Path of the voice.

Muin is a complex few, with multiple meanings. This is made even more entangled by McManus' assertion that there are two variant readings of Morainn mac Moin's kenning. These multiple layers of meaning certainly reflect the divinatory meaning of the few as an entwining, entangling force. The first of mac Moin's kennings ('strongest in exertion') and CúChulainn's both refer to the meaning of the word muin as 'upper part of the back, neck'. Mac ind Oc's kenning ('proverb of slaughter') refers to a different word muin, which means 'wile, ruse, trick, or treachery'. This word is used in reference to Bricriu in the Irish tales, a Celtic Loki-figure, which should not surprise us. Finally, the alternate reading of Morainn mac Moin, ('most noble goodliness') refers to yet another Old Irish word muin, whose meaning is 'love, esteem'. A suitably tangled web of meanings for a multi-dimensional few.

Tree:

The vine is the plant later attributed to muin. It is of course cultivated to produce wine, whose effect has long been associated with the Otherworld. The vine is also significant for the intricate interlacing vine motifs which are so prominent in Celtic art. These symbolise the intricacies of the subjective world made manifest and objective.

Deities and Heroes:

The god of muin is Manannán mac Lir. This deity has strong associations with the sea, and is Lord of the Underworld (which can be said to lie beneath the sea). Manannán expresses all aspects of human consciousness in his complex being. On one level, he lives in a mighty fortress atop a mountain in the Isle of Man, signifying man's conscious awareness, his knowledge of solid things in this world. On the other hand, he lives in the Underworld realm of the sidhe, representing the dark and mysterious depths of the subconscious,

111

which must be plumbed by those seeking mastery of self. Both realms meet in Manannán.

Also corresponding is Morfessa, the "Master of Great Knowledge", who rules the Otherworldly city of Falias in the north.

The goddess associated with muin is the Mórrígan, whose name means "Great Queen", or "Queen of the Phantoms". She is the embodiment of a goddess-triad called the Mórrígu. These are sinister goddesses of war, death, magic and eroticism, overshadowing the battlefield. For the heroic, they can represent those rare moments of lucidity, when a crisis point is reached and all worlds become one in the intensity of the experience. The Mórrígan is the dark and dangerous, but rapid, route to self-knowledge and magical power.

The Mórrígan persisted into the early Christian era, taking shape in the minds of the Celts once again as Morgan Le Fay in the Arthurian tales. This goddess is willing to teach, but her lessons are hard and ruthless and come at a great price. Nevertheless, she represents another side of muin, the interweaving of the inner and outer worlds in a unified model.

Morgan Le Fay is not the only Arthurian archetype to exemplify muin, as the mighty Merlin also corresponds to this ogham, subtly manipulating people and events until his inner vision of the Land unified under a British King is made real. In Merlin, we see the perfect example of applying the M-few in practice. Under his tutelage, the King and the Land become one, and his dream becomes reality, even if only for a little while.

A similar figure is found in the great druid Mathgen in the Irish tales.

Another heroic correspondence is Mongán, who is the "son" or incarnation – similar to the Indian concept of the avatar – of Manannán mac Lir. Not only this, he was also said to be the reincarnation of Finn mac Cumhaill. He is the archetype of the heroic human who braves the Underworld to gain magical knowledge.

Colour:

The colour of muin is "variegated", rather than any single colour or shade. This attribution reflects the complex intertwining

112

and multi-faceted nature of the few.

Bird:

    The bird attributed to muin is the titmouse, an extremely nimble and agile small bird, capable of flying great distances, but most often seen flitting from one tree to another.

Arts and Crafts / Profession:

    "Soldiering" is the profession of the M-few. This may represent a literal military profession, or those on the spiritual path of the warrior. Such mysteries were more pervasive in times gone by than they are in western society today, but the attitude and courage of the warrior must still be cultivated, certainly if the mysteries of the Mórrígan are sought after.

    Quite appropriately for this ogham, the great questions of life do remain a battleground, but they have shifted to an inner plane and are less immediately obvious in consequence.

Numerology:

    Celtic lore ascribes no emphatic significance to the number eleven, but it is interesting to note that it is formed by two number 1s side by side, as if to emphasise the interplay between two worlds within muin.

Divinatory Meanings:

    Muin represents the intertwining of the conscious and subconscious strata of the psyche, allowing a deeper and much more complex perspective on life. The process is a gentle and cumulative one. Logic and rational thought are not cast out, but instead are gradually supplemented with intuition and inspiration. It is an extension of one's limits into new areas, a new experience of the interplay between inner and outer, upper and lower.

    This interlacing of various worlds - with the centre of self (the féin) always the centre around which all else revolves - has its operative uses in two main ways. One the one hand, if the querent has problem in the everyday world, he/she may expect insights and guidance on these issues to arise from within, allowing new creative possibilities which may not have ordinarily been evident. In this way, the deep creative faculties of the mind may bring their influence to bear in many areas of life, so that the subjective layers of the querent begin to reshape the outside world, becoming objectively manifest. On the other hand, the querent becomes increasingly sensitive to those experiences and stimuli in the objective sphere which have a resonance with his/her innermost being, and thus knowledge and development of self are enhanced by taking these objective stimuli onboard.

The danger in the M-few is that of losing the distinction between objective and subjective levels of perception, and confusing the two. There is a difference between being able to see and manipulate the interlinkings between the two (positive) and becoming unable to differentiate and allowing boundaries to blur and become indistinct (negative). In the former case, the querent is empowered and insightful; in the latter case, the querent is unfocused and confused.

The Fifths:

Muin in Mide	Inwardness in Sovereignty	Dignity (+)
Muin in Seis	Inwardness in Harmony	Subtlety (+)
Muin in Fis	Inwardness in Learning	Modesty (+)
Muin in Cath	Inwardness in Conflict	Pride (+)
Muin in Blath	Inwardness in Prosperity	Prestige (+)

GORT – Field
Development

Description:

Gort represents the alchemical process, the transformation of

The Book of Ogham

base materials into intricate and wonderful objects. As such, it governs all craftsmanship that is guided by the combination of skill and will.

By obvious analogy, the G-few also refers to the more divine art of the transformation and development of the self by a process of willed change.

Word Oghams:
Word Ogham of Morainn mac Moin: Sweetest grass.
Word Ogham of Maic ind Oc: Suitable place for cows.
Word Ogham of CúChulainn: Sating of multitudes.

All of the kennings point to the meaning of 'field, grass, pasture'. The Old Irish word gort is cognate with Welsh gorth, meaning 'garden, enclosure'. The act of enclosing a field or garden and using the space for either grazing livestock or growing plants is not inconsistent with the few's divinatory meaning of 'development'. McManus suggests that the later attribution of ivy and honeysuckle to the few may derive from the 'greenest pasture' kenning, since both are evergreens.

Tree:
The ivy is the plant later attributed to the G-few. It is a long-lived and hardy plant, which climbs over all surfaces. It shares some of the intricacy of the vine, which is attributed to the preceding few, but in gort that intricacy is expressed on a more exterior level, in shaping an object to its highest developmental potential.

The ivy also symbolises the feminine, as holly represents the masculine. This is expressed in the archaic carol, "The Holly and the Ivy".

Deities and Heroes:
The god associated with gort is Goibhniu, the smith-god. His is the skill of metal-working, of producing beautiful and intricate work. The Celts were wonderful workers of metals, just how wonderful can still be seen in museums in those places where they were established. There is almost a mystical quality about the transformation of base

115

substances into something precious and beautiful in the hands of master craftsmen.

The Cymric equivalent of Goibhniu was the god Gofannon, also a smith, but his tales are now largely lost to us.

Another corresponding Cymric deity would be Gwydion, who was a shoemaker, and thus similarly the maker of something useful and beautiful out of the application of skill upon base substances.

Colour:

The colour associated with the G-few is blue. This is traditionally a royal colour and the colour of the sky, thus representative of divinity. It is also the colour with which many Celtic warriors adorned themselves before battle, painting their skins with woad, part of the ritualistic process of transformation with which they prepared themselves to fight and perhaps to die.

Bird:

The bird corresponding with gort is the swan. This immediately brings to mind the well-known folk tale of the "Ugly Duckling", which was initially ridiculed because of its ungainly appearance, but was finally the envy of its fellows when it transformed into a beautiful swan and outshone them all. It is a regal bird.

Arts and Crafts / Profession:

As befitting the other attributions of this few, the profession attributed to gort is that of metal-working. The emphasis is upon the transformative principle, upon creating a finished product from raw materials. As such, there is also a correspondence with any craft which employs skills and materials in such a manner, and also with chemistry and other processes of mixing and adjusting substances in order to transform them.

Numerology:

Gort is the twelfth ogham, and twelve is a number of completion. There are twelve months in the year, the Earth is encircled by twelve zodiacal signs (which were known to the Celts), and twelve warriors sat around a king (both in Ireland - as described in the palace built for Bricriu's feast - and also in Arthurian symbolism.)

Divinatory Meanings:

Gort is the principle of transformation from a base condition to a higher state. It is exemplified by fine craftsmanship, which uses the application of the focused will, the proper tools, and hard won skills over a period of time to painstakingly create items of intricate beauty and value.

As such, the few corresponds with any attempts to use one's skills to move the tone of a given situation from a lower level to a higher. It is the ability to make the most of the tools and the position at hand to create something perfect and satisfying.

This few also obviously represents the development of the soul, and the process remains the same: such transformations of self are only lastingly and beautifully wrought by long and intense self-examination, an objective view of one's own character strengths and weaknesses, and the application of skills to nurture growth in the right way. This is a time-consuming process, and a potentially dangerous one if done ham-fistedly (the clumsiness that would mar the appearance of a silver bowl can also leave mental scars). However, it is the highest and most noble of human activities, to aspire to express the divine spark within oneself and to seek to bring that essence and potential onto manifestation.

There is one major danger in the G-few, which is easily overlooked. It may be noticed that in all of the above descriptions of the few's meaning, I have left out the single most important point. It is necessary to have vision, to know what one is trying to create. The metallurgist who begins tracing intricate patterns on a piece of bronze is a fool if he has not previously decided what those patterns are intended to represent. But there is a real danger of losing sight of the purpose of the transformational process by getting so caught up in the process itself that we forget why we are really doing it.

The Book of Ogham

Gort in Mide	Development in Sovereignty	Development (+)
Gort in Seis	Development in Harmony	Attainment (+)
Gort in Fis	Development in Learning	Education (+)
Gort in Cath	Development in Conflict	Ruin (-)
Gort in Blath	Development in Prosperity	Futility (-)

GÉTAL - (Act of) Wounding / Slaying
Harmony

Description:

Gétal is a few which stresses the harmonisation of the inner and outer worlds. As such, it governs aesthetics and artistic appreciation in general, as well as certain types of creative endeavour. It has a certain affinity with the famous Hermetic maxim which says, "That which is above is like that which is below, and that which is below is like that which is above, to achieve the wonders of the One Thing."

The few encourage a resonance between subjective and objective levels of being, often perceived as an increased incidence of meaningful synchronicities in life.

Word Oghams:

Word Ogham of Morainn mac Moin: Sustenance of a leech.

Word Ogham of Maic ind Oc: Raiment of physicians.

Word Ogham of CúChulainn: Beginning of slaying.

'Sustenance of a leech' and 'raiment of a physician' are both suggestive of blood: the leech feeds upon it and the physician is coated in it during surgery. This meaning is obviously echoed in 'beginning of slaying'. The meaning of the ogham name seems to be 'act of wounding' and the Old Irish word is cognate with the Welsh

118

gwanu, meaning 'pierce, stab'. The later attribution of the reed, fern or bracken to this few also seems to derive from the kennings due to their many healing uses and blood-staunching.

Tree:

The plant later associated with this ogham is the reed, which grows straight up out of marshy and wet land. This symbolises the harmonisation of forces: it is green life emerging from a watery bed; it is vertical growth from a horizontal plane. It enshrines the importance of boundaries and "in-betweens" (being neither of the land nor the water) to the Celtic mind.

Deities and Heroes:

The sound expressed by the GG-few is an archaic one (similar to nasal "ng"), which goes back to thee very roots of the ogham and was no longer in everyday use in the times in which the records which we have were written.

As such, there are deities or heroes known to us whose names actually begin with this sound. There are several beginning with the N or G sound, however, which have a certain correspondence and may be used here.

Colour:

The colour associated with gétal is green. Green has always been regarded as a harmonious and soothing colour in most schools of thought in colour therapy. It is stimulating, but in a gentle and calming way.

Bird:

The goose is the bird associated with gétal. As with the reed attribution, it is a creature comfortable both on land and in the water, and thus it emphasises the harmonisation of different realms.

Arts and Crafts / Profession:

The profession of this few is "modeling", as in modeling something out of clay. It might better be understood as "designing" in today's terminology. It is the act of visualising something in the mind's eye and shaping its form in the outer world. This link between inner and outer is the crux of the few.

Numerology:

The number of gétal is thirteen, and its symbolism is linked to that of the previous few. The number thirteen signifies the king sitting surrounded by twelve warriors, or the world encircled by the zodiacal signs. With gort, the previous few, the emphasis was upon twelve, and the complete cycle. With gétal, however, the thirteenth unit in the centre of the wheel is emphasised, thus highlighting the polarity and resonance between the inner and outer once again.

Divinatory Meanings:

Gétal recognises that the subjective world within and the objective world without, while distinct from one another, nevertheless may influence one another, and that the querent can learn from both.

This is quite distinct from the meaning of muin, which stresses the intertwinings between conscious and subconscious levels of the psyche, and the interactions between self and not-self. Gétal instead seeks to harmonise the and synchronise the inner and outer worlds, making them run in parallel, whilst recognising the two as separate continua.

In doing so, a resonance is developed between the psyche and the world it inhabits, so that the vision of the querent is reflected by manifestations of a synchronistic nature in the outside world. Everything just seems to "click into place" and opportunities open up and are there to be taken. This is harmonisation, not identification, the distinction is essential.

To quote an example from personal experience, when researching for this book, I wanted to obtain a copy of Celtic Heritage by Alwyn and Brinley Rees. The very weekend I determined to do so, I walked into a small second-hand bookshop and it was the first title I saw, sat on a shelf at my eye level, directly opposite the door. My mind and the world were synching closely together that day.

There is one important prerequisite before the GG-few can

be successfully used, and this is that you must understand the way in which the world works before you can reliably and consistently resonate your inner vision with it. This is hard work. It is necessary to construct an inner mental model of reality and the way in which it operates. Chapters 2 and 3 should help in this regard.

A danger in gétal occurs when the psyche has established no such model for itself and may be subject to random influences from "outside", or is badly affected by something the individual was not prepared for.

The Fifths:

Gétal in Mide	Harmony in Sovereignty	Stability (+)
Gétal in Seis	Harmony in Harmony	Harmony (+)
Gétal in Fis	Harmony in Learning	Beauty (+)
Gétal in Cath	Harmony in Conflict	Rest (+)
Gétal in Blath	Harmony in Prosperity	Good Manners (+)

SRAIB or STRAIF - Sulphur
Control / Coercion

Description:

Straif is considered to be an unlucky few, with malevolent associations. It implies that control is being exerted upon a person, object, or situation from an outside source. As such, it is a focus of coercion.

There is something manipulative and devious about the Z-few. This is the few of malevolent magic, as coll is that of the benevolent kind.

Word Oghams:
Word Ogham of Morainn mac Moin: Strongest reddening.

The Book of Ogham

Word Ogham of Maic ind Oc: Increase of secrets.
Word Ogham of CúChulainn: Seeking of clouds.

The ogham name refers to sulphur and this and its chemical reactions is obviously referred to in the 'strongest reddening' kenning. Its use may also be alluded to in the 'seeking of clouds' kenning, although this might be more akin to Maic ind Oc's meaning, which we will discuss shortly. In such a case, the clouds would refer to concealment and the kenning could therefore be considered a statement akin to 'Seek After the Mysteries'! 'Increase of secrets' is definitely a reference to magic and mysticism. The Old Irish phrase is 'Mórad rún': the word rún, here translated as 'secret', has the same meaning as rune in Germanic languages.

Tree:

The blackthorn is attributed to straif, a twisted and thorny shrub which is very common in Britain's hedgerows. This wood is the blasting rod of the malevolent magician. It is often carried as a walking stick, club, or weapon. The sharpened magical weapon used to injure effigies of one's enemies is traditionally of blackthorn.

Deities and Heroes:

No deity names begin with this ogham, but there are some aspects associated with those listed under the S-few. In some respects, the darker, hidden aspects of the Celtic deities may all be attributed here.

Colour:

The colour of the Z-few is "bright". This is a glaring brightness that disorients and dazzles the eyes.

Bird:

The thrush is attributed to the Z-few. It is a very common small bird, most often noted by its song.

Arts and Crafts / Profession:

The profession traditionally attributed to straif is "deer-stalking". In contemporary terms, it may apply to any profession in which an individual advances himself by stealth and cunning, by waiting until an advantage can be taken and then striking. It is the exercise of vigilance and precision from a position of concealed strength.

Numerology:

Straif is the fourteenth ogham. The number fourteen itself has no specifically Celtic symbolism attached to it. It is 2 X 7, and thus carries tones of duality and of comprehensiveness. It is also the fourth ogham in the third aicme. As such, it corresponds with all four directions, surrounding the centre. This may suggest the theme of control by outside influences which pervades this few, the sense of being enclosed and trapped.

Divinatory Meanings:

Straif refers to those powers which control and constrain us which have their origin outside of ourselves. More often than not, this is a negative force, limiting personal freedom and choice. Certainly, whenever the few falls in a divinatory context, it can always be assumed to refer to such a scenario, with the querent being controlled – very possibly without even realising it – and persuaded to follow somebody else's agenda instead of following his/her own path.

Very often, the main key in transforming a situation involving straif is simply to become aware of its influence and to identify the controlling force. Once recognised, its insidious power is lost and it can be resisted and made allowance for, or – sometimes – even accepted and worked with consciously, on your own terms. In such a case, the element of choice is restored to the querent.

Straif may also sometimes herald a more complex situation, a conflict of interests, where perceived duty urges action of one sort, but personal ethics urge an entirely different course of action. These struggles can have far reaching consequences. No easy answers can be given in such a situation, only facts to be weighed in the balance by the individual.

Straif is not all bad, of course, but is most certainly dangerous for those unprepared for its somewhat devious power. In some instances, it is necessary for someone to assume control in order to resolve a situation, but care must be taken to keep all above board and transparent, for the few's more malicious effects can ensnare even the best motives.

The Fifths:

Straif in Mide	Control in Sovereignty	Stewardship (+)
Straif in Seis	Control in Harmony	Vehemence (-)
Straif in Fis	Control in Learning	Testing (-)
Straif in Cath	Control in Conflict	Capture (-)
Straif in Blath	Control in Prosperity	Debt (-)

RUISE – Reddening
Change

Description:
     Ruise is a few of change. It is a recognition that nothing remains the same, but passes through a cycle of changes. People are born, grow old and die. Time passes and the world is changed. In some respects, this few can be seen as fate, i.e. those times and circumstances in life which are inevitable and must be passed through.
     Unlike gort, which refers to a process of willed change and development, ruise refers to changes and cycles which occur outside the confines of self, but nonetheless impinge upon it. The focus of the few is upon the individual's response to and use of these changes as it passes through them. Are they used as catalysts for growth or do we fear and shun change, shrinking as we do so?

Word Oghams:
Word Ogham of Morainn mac Moin: Most intense blushing.

The Book of Ogham

Word Ogham of Maic ind Oc: Reddening of faces.
Word Ogham of CúChulainn: Glow of anger.

All three kennings point to redness or reddening, most specifically the reddening of a face in response to some emotional stimulus. The ogham name itself means 'red'. The later attribution of the elder tree to the few is as a consequence of this original meaning of redness, which is reflected in the red berries of the tree.

Tree:

The elder is the tree of ruise. This is because its red berries were used in cosmetics for their blushing effect.

Elder is considered a bad tree to burn, reputedly bringing the devil into the house. This is derived from the Christian belief that the cross of the crucifixion was of elder wood. It may have its roots in earlier Celtic belief, however; on the Isle of Man the elder is referred to as the tramman tree, and the Manx people will never lay a blade to it nor harm it in any way, for in Manx lore this tree is a gate to the Otherworld and sacred to the sidhe.

Deities and Heroes:

The god most closely associated with ruise is Ruadh Rofessa. This is another name for the Dagda, meaning "the Red-one who knows all".

Rigru Roisclethan is a queen of the Otherworld and one of the goddesses representing Irish sovereignty. This also accords with the goddess Rigantona, whose name simply means "the great queen". Of all the goddesses whose names begin with the R-sound, however, the one who best embodies the qualities of change immanent within this few is Rhiannon, the equine goddess who is the daughter of the king of the Underworld.

The heroic attribution is Ragallach. He was one of the Irish kings, who ordered his daughter slain when it was prophesied that he would die at her hand. She survived in hiding, however, and later became her father's concubine by a twist of fate. These sometimes bizarre shifts and changes in fortune to follow a fated pattern are typical of the R-few.

The Book of Ogham

Colour:

The colour of ruise is red. The kennings for the few refer to blushing. A person blushes when embarrassed or caught off guard, and this kind of response is typical of the changes represented by this ogham, which precipitates us out of an existing situation into a new one, an unknown quantity.

For those who grasp the lessons of this few and apply its "blushing" symbolism in a hearty and positive manner, this vibrant colour is also indicative of a deep love for life and an eagerness to experience it and live it to the full.

Bird:

The bird associated with ruise is the rook, a member of the crow family. Although very social, these birds are adept at hiding food and other treasures and remembering their location afterwards, when needed.

Arts and Crafts / Profession:

The profession associated with this ogham is that of the "middle-man", who dispenses goods and services to a wider public, acting as go-between. As such, it is the catalytic element in any human transaction, making available things that might otherwise have been difficult to acquire, thus accelerating the rate of change and progress.

Numerology:

The number fifteen is attributed to this few, standing at the end of the third aicme, completing three rows of five. in terms of the cosmological model, it has five strokes and thus represents a universal absolute. It is also the final consonant in the ogham series.

All of this goes to suggest that the cycles of change are immutable cosmic laws which cannot be circumvented. Change = stability.

Divinatory Meanings:

Ruise is the realisation that all things change. The world around us changes, people are born and die, new things are made and

The Book of Ogham

old things break apart. Even our own bodies are completely replaced on a cellular level every few years.

The mental trauma many people feel with this few is that we become attached to familiar things and are afraid of having to accustom ourselves to new things. But it is inevitable that life is full of such changes. We cannot remain a child, we grow up. Play is left behind, we must be educated. School is left behind, we must work. Marriage and children follow, then retirement and death. Life follows its inexorable cycle, and within these greater cycles, the smaller, more personal, wheels of fate are turning.

The question of ruise is whether we are swept along by these cycles from crisis to crisis, or whether we make use of them to enrich life. Every change in life is an opportunity for new knowledge, achievement and joy. Every challenge thrown down is a new victory to be won. There is no point in fighting the inevitable, but you can liberate yourself from tyranny by using changes by using changes in your environment and circumstances to explore and express yourself more fully, in ways that may have been inappropriate or impossible previously. Life can be play.

We must come to terms with the changing world and assume responsibility for our own responses to, and uses of, it. To fail to do so is to be swept along regardless, helpless and impotent, or worse still to succeed for a short time in holding back change and succumb to the numbness of stasis instead, cut off from our surroundings and fellows.

The Fifths:

Ruise in Mide	Change in Sovereignty	Maturity (+)
Ruise in Seis	Change in Harmony	New Knowledge (+)
Ruise in Fis	Change in Learning	Advancement (+)
Ruise in Cath	Change in Conflict	Survival (+)
Ruise in Blath	Change in Prosperity	Generosity (+)

The Book of Ogham

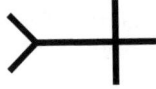

AILM – Pine-Tree
Objectivity (Sovereignty)

Description:
    Ailm is the first of the vowels in the ogham classification, and as with beithe, the initial consonant in the series (and indeed the first of all the ogham fews), it signifies birth and beginnings.
    Ailm is a very lofty conception, representing the powers of objectivity and sovereignty. As such, it may seem aloof and remote at times, but from its lofty perspective it is able to effectively embody the principles of justice, fairness and right action.

Word Oghams:
Word Ogham of Morainn mac Moin: Loudest groan.
Word Ogham of Maic ind Oc: Beginning of an answer.
Word Ogham of CúChulainn: Beginning of calling.
    All three of the kennings relating to this few refer to its sound ("Ah") rather than to its meaning, or specifically the beginning of its sound. This may be significant given the divinatory interpretations relating to beginnings. It is difficult to assert the original meaning of ailm, but the tree attribution of 'pine' or 'fir' may be correct, as the name is used in this context in the King and Hermit poem, which reads 'caine ailmi ardom-peitet': 'beautiful are the pines which make music for me'.

Tree:
    The tree attributed to the A-few is the pine or fir. This tree is taken to symbolise birth, and there was a Celtic tradition of blessing a mother and baby with a torch of fir wood. Significantly, ailm was also the name given by the Irish to the Mediterranean palm tree, which is the tree of birth in that region.
    The shape of the tree also suggests the sovereign aspects of

128

this few, as it is very upstanding and lordly. The cones stand upright on the tree, and old trees may grow several large branches which turn sharply upwards alongside the bole and vie with the central stem.

Deities and Heroes:

It is Aedh, the primeval fire god, who is attributed to this few. He presides over the great fire festivals which mark the passing of the year, and thus represents an objective measure of time and responsibility.

The goddess associated with the A-few is Aine, who is either the wife or daughter of the sea god, Manannán mac Lir. She is another goddess who represents the sovereignty of Ireland.

Interestingly, in these two figures we find the primeval dichotomy between fire and water.

The heroic figure attributed to the few is Art, one of the ancient Irish kings. He is said to have reigned from 220 to 254 CE, but his tales contain many obviously mythic strands which exemplify the socio-magical role of sovereignty in the ancient Celtic tradition.

The same is equally true of the later Arthur, king of the Britons, who is still the archetypal figure of heroic British kingship, his tales teaching the mystery that the king and the land are one.

Colour:

The colour of this few is piebald. This is a very natural and in many ways unremarkable patterning. Objectivity must encompass the great and the small, favouring no one thing over any other thing, but viewing all with a measured eye.

Bird:

The lapwing is the bird attributed to the A-few. It is a bird of bold colours and a long, wispy crest, enhancing its kingly aspect.

Arts and Crafts / Profession:

The profession associated with the A-few is that of king or sovereign. In the modern world, this may represent anybody in a position of authority who may exercise a sovereign power, whether in a nation, corporation, club or society.

Numerology:
The number sixteen is a significant one in Irish lore. The Lebor Gabala lists sixteen triads of the Tuatha Dé Danann, and kin could be counted to the sixteenth generation. The division of land into sixteenths is also not unknown, as each of the four directions around the centre are subdivided into quarters of their own. This implies a sense of comprehensiveness in measuring to established boundaries in all directions, both spatial and temporal, and accords well with the meaning of the few. This is the ordered realm over which sovereignty is exercised.

As the first few in this aicme, ailm also resonates with a sense of beginning, of birth.

Divinatory Meanings:
The A-few implies that an objective eye is used to establish boundaries and to order the world around you into a coherent and productive one. This process of bringing order to a chaotic cosmos is the first step on the path of enlightenment. Where once chaos reigned the sovereign will imposes discipline and a sense of priorities.

The true sovereign here, of course, is the individual psyche, which must bring order to its own world, as each human being who wishes to be successful in life must take steps to introduce order and cohesion. It is not enough to be tossed and bruised by chance factors in life, it is necessary to take control and to introduce measures for dealing with life and actively taking control of it and steering where you want it to go. This is a very demanding task, which is why it is compared with the task of kings.

Once self-ordering is established, the will may extend its influence over an increasing portion of the world around it. The danger here will always be that of attempting to run before you can walk. As the A-few stresses, sovereign power depends absolutely upon an objective viewpoint. Facts must be fully known and impartially evaluated in order for any action to be successful. Good organisational skills are essential to this ogham.

The Book of Ogham

In a divinatory context, the appearance of this few might signify that some new responsibility and opportunity may present itself to the querent. As such, it is a warning to act with forethought and due consideration. This is a few which brings great rewards when properly applied in a balanced manner, but can bring disaster if mishandled. We are probably all aware of the chaos that can be caused by bad management and lack of organisation.

The Fifths:

Ailm in Mide	Objectivity in Sovereignty	Sovereignty (+)
Ailm in Seis	Objectivity in Harmony	Discovery (+)
Ailm in Fis	Objectivity in Learning	Mastery (+)
Ailm in Cath	Objectivity in Conflict	Strategy (+)
Ailm in Blath	Objectivity in Prosperity	Originality (+)

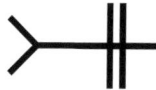

ONN – Ash-Tree
Wisdom (Synthesis)

Description:

The O-few represents the process of gathering together all manner of knowledge, perspectives, and experiences, and from this gathered mass producing a synthesis, which is understanding. Wisdom is derived from the careful and considered weighing of all available knowledge, which produces a higher perspective.

Word Oghams:
Word Ogham of Morainn mac Moin: Wounder of horses.
Word Ogham of Maic ind Oc: Smoothest of craftsmanship.
Word Ogham of CúChulainn: Sustaining of warrior-bands.

There are variant readings for Morainn mac Moin's kenning: some sources have 'congnaid ech' ('wounder of horses') and others

131

The Book of Ogham

have 'congnamaid ech' ('helper of horses'). McManus suggests that 'wounder of horses' is the earlier of the two. Onn was the original Old Irish word for 'ash-tree' (later replaced by uinnius); onnaid later came to mean 'the wheel-rim of a chariot'. Since ash, being strong and pliant, was used for horse-whips, this marks the 'wounder' variant as the original. 'Smoothest of craftsmanship' is easily attributed to ash and 'sustaining of warrior-bands' refers to the use of ash as spear shafts. The attribution of furze to this few came much later, when the interpreters of the kennings had forgotten that onn was an ancient name for ash.

Tree:

In later times, the ash, which was originally attributed to onn, became associated with nin and the gorse or furze became the shrub associated with the O-few. This is a spiny evergreen with small yellow blossoms (as with wisdom, the ingathering may be painful, but the blossom is sweet). It makes a good food for animals after it has been ground or burned to destroy the sharp thorns.

It was a British custom to include a spray of gorse in the bridal bouquet, giving rise to an old saying that "when the gorse is out of bloom, kissing's out of season".

Deities and Heroes:

The god most clearly associated with onn is Ogma, the inventor of ogham. His mythology is largely covered in the first chapter, but briefly to recap, he is the god of strength and of eloquence, thus a good symbol for wisdom (which wisdom is, of course, encoded in the oghams he created).

The hero of the O-few is Oisin, one of the warrior poets numbered among the Fianna. He spent three hundred years in the Land of Youth with his Otherworldly lover, Niamh. He returned to this world on a horse given him by Niamh, but was warned not to allow his foot to touch the earth. However, his foot did touch the ground accidentally as his horse slipped and his missing years caught up with him and he became a very aged man. True to the meaning of this few, Oisin ensured that the wisdom of the Fianna was preserved in

The Book of Ogham

words through the ages by relating their history to St Patrick before he died.

Colour:

The colour of the O-few is dun, that sort of muddy colour that is obtained when other colours are all mixed together. This symbolises the ingathering and synthesis of information before wisdom can be attained.

Bird:

The scrat is the bird associated with onn.

Arts and Crafts / Profession:

Harvesting is the profession attributed to this few, and is an excellent symbolic representation of its action. Seeds are sown in order to reap a future crop. They are tended with hard work, cultivated with skill and perseverance, finally to yield a harvest, which is then used to sustain and enrich life.

Numerology:

Onn is the seventeenth few, and the symbolism for this number follows naturally from that of ailm, the sixteenth few. Whereas the number sixteen represents the ordering of the land / cosmos and the establishment of boundaries, the number seventeen presides over that ordering from the central point, as wisdom is won through the process of establishing order.

Divinatory Meanings:

Onn represents the attainment of wisdom by the ingathering and synthesis of valuable and pertinent things. One of the other symbols for this few is the beehive, for honey is a sweet substance which is the result of hard work and gathering by bees.

Most particularly in a divinatory context, the few refers to drawing together all of the different strands of your life and deliberately dedicating them to your chosen goal. In this way, wisdom is won and all of your resources work together instead of pulling in

The Book of Ogham

different directions. Wisdom is a numinous quality which is only attained when a certain quantity and quality of work has been done previously, allowing a firm foundation from which intuition may spring. This may also open the possibility of a divine wisdom, with insights obtainable from Otherworld sources.

The work of gathering wisdom should be done for its own sake, with care and with dedication; wisdom springs from the work itself, from the very act of doing.

One of the biggest dangers of this few is winning wisdom and then simply basking in it and doing nothing with it. Such 'wisdom' is sterile and ultimately proves foolish. The other danger is getting so wrapped up in the process of gathering that one forgets what it is all for; a sense of purpose is essential to true wisdom.

The Fifths:

Onn in Mide	Wisdom in Sovereignty	Guidance (+)
Onn in Seis	Wisdom in Harmony	Rulership (+)
Onn in Fis	Wisdom in Learning	Passion (+)
Onn in Cath	Wisdom in Conflict	Change (+)
Onn in Blath	Wisdom in Prosperity	Security (+)

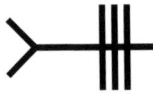

UR, UIR – Earth, Soil; Grave
Gateway / Passion

Description:

The U-few is representative of acts of passion, and of the drive to adventure which often accompanies such emotions. It also symbolises a gateway, opening up new opportunities and new life experiences. Passion is one of those peculiarly intense states of mind which seems to being such gateways into being.

134

The Book of Ogham

Word Oghams:
Word Ogham of Morainn mac Moin: In cold dwellings.
Word Ogham of Maic ind Oc: Propagation of plants.
Word Ogham of CúChulainn: Shroud of a dead man.

The ogham name means 'earth, clay, soil' and this is clearly indicated by all three kennings. The earth is figured here both as the fertile ground from which new plants spring and also the burial place of the dead. From cradle to grave. This fits neatly with the divinatory meaning of 'a gateway', as new life comes out of the ground as the dead return to it, passing to and from the Underworld.

Tree:

Heather is the plant later associated with the U-few, and has long been linked to acts of passion. Red heather at midsummer is a sign of passion, whereas white heather is a lucky sign and a protection against acts of passion.

In Wales, heather ale is brewed as a restorative.

Deities and Heroes:

In Irish mythology, úr relates to Uscias, the master of knowledge who dwells in the Otherworldly city of Finias in the south. It was he who gave the sword to Nuada.

Uathach was the daughter of Scathach, who taught the arts of war to CúChulainn. It was Uathach who arranged for CúChulainn to enter Scathach's school and she later became the hero's mistress after he killed her lover. Thus Uathach embodies both the passion and gateway aspects of the few (she is CúChulainn's lover and his means of access).

Colour:

The colour allocated to this few is "resinous". It is the inner life of things. There is also a certain sexual symbolism here which is highly appropriate to the few.

Bird:

The lark is attributed to úr, a bird which often escapes

The Book of Ogham

danger by running along the ground, even though it is a swift flyer; it is cunning enough to use the contours of the ground and foliage cover to conceal its escape. It attracts its mate with beautiful song, which is also pleasant to the human ear.

Arts and Crafts / Profession:
The profession of the U-few is "brasswork". This is metal-working skill, as also attributed to the G-few, but here it is specifically allocated to the more delicate and intricate domestic uses, creating objects of great beauty for reasons as much aesthetic as utilitarian.

Numerology:
Ur is the eighteenth few. As such, it is twice nine and partakes of the qualities of that number, i.e. of the sovereign self in the centre of its world. It also has a significance of its own, however, which follows on from the values and meanings of the sixteenth and seventeenth numbers. The eighteenth thing, person or object is sometimes seen as being that most perfect, the one that surpasses all the others and can achieve that which they cannot do. It is the one that stands outside of and superior to the cosmological model of sixteen and seventeen and thus wields a power that the mere worldly numbers cannot. For example, it is on the eighteenth attempt that Fergus succeeds in uprooting a tree; only the eighteenth chariot – the king's own – is good enough for CúChulainn.

Divinatory Meanings:
Ur encompasses all aspects of passion, including the dreamy and romantic. There is a fire within it too, however, for when a subject is aflame with passion, the conscious and subconscious levels of the psyche become united as one in their desire. Passion acts as a vivifying and unifying force upon consciousness and it is in this way that it becomes a gateway, firstly to inner realms of the self but also to new opportunities in life.
When the soul is thus focused and unified, the exterior world is more easily malleable to its influence, and thus opens itself up to the querent. Hoe many tales and (nowadays) movies have been based

136

The Book of Ogham

upon this premise, when an individual casts away his/her old life in the name of passion and makes a completely new start. They marvel then at the wonders and opportunities the world has to offer. But those wonders and opportunities were there all along; it is the intensity of passion which renders them noticeable now and offers them as real gateways for the future.

It is only in the rut of everyday routine and the crushing inertial existence which contemporary western life expects of its subjects that we lose sight of these great treasures. When this few appears in a divinatory reading, or is used in a magical process, it is usually a call to open up sufficient room for passion to manifest in life, so that the querent may truly live and cease merely existing. This is a vivacious few.

There is, as always, a danger. The danger with úr is that of aspiring to fantastic and impractical dreams which can never be realised, or of giving up everything to embark on a wild goose chase. Passion must remain precisely focused, and when we chase after our dreams it must be with full awareness, good preparation and planning, and hard work, as well as a twinkle in our eye.

The Fifths:

Ur in Mide	Passion in Sovereignty	Inspiration (+)
Ur in Seis	Passion in Harmony	Disturbance (-)
Ur in Fis	Passion in Learning	Eagerness (+)
Ur in Cath	Passion in Conflict	Fury (+)
Ur in Blath	Passion in Prosperity	Greed (-)

The Book of Ogham

>─║║║║

ÉO – Salmon > EDAD
Overcoming

Description:
Edad is a symbol of determination in the face of adversity. It is the cultivation and use of indomitable inner strength to overcome any obstacles which stand in one's way. As such, it is a somewhat martial sign, strong both in defence and attack, but always with a view to the victory of consciousness over non-consciousness.

Word Oghams:
Word Ogham of Morainn mac Moin: Discerning tree.
Word Ogham of Maic ind Oc: Exchange of friends.
Word Ogham of CúChulainn: Brother of birch.

There is considerable difficulty in interpreting the kennings for the E-few and in discovering its original name. The key may lie in Maic ind Oc's kenning, 'exchange of friends'. Which friends? The friends in question are the words éo meaning 'yew tree' and éo meaning 'salmon'. 'Discerning tree' could refer to the use of yew rods in divination, which – through the prior exchange – could be interpreted as the salmon of knowledge. The final kenning, 'brother of birch' is ambiguous, though commentators point to 'salmon' as the meaning in all three cases, which sits well with the name of the few and the overall tone of the ogham's meanings. 'Salmon' is thus the most likely original name for this few unless further information should come to light.

Tree:
Aspen is the tree attributed to the E-few, and was often used to make shields, which are used to overcome the might of one's enemy.

Irish coffin makers used to use a traditional measuring stick

The Book of Ogham

made of aspen, called a fe, to measure the body for its coffin and grave. This symbolises the overcoming of death.

The aspen was also used in divination, by listening to the sounds made by the wind rustling through its leaves.

Deities and Heroes:

A divine figure associated with this few is the master of wisdom named Esras, who dwelt in the Otherworldly city of Gorias in the east. He gave a spear to the god Lugh.

Edad probably accords most closely with the goddess Ériu, who is the goddess of sovereignty, and from whom the name of the land of Ireland is derived. This name is also cognate with the first element in the names Iran and Aryan and the Germanic Yrmin, all having to do with those who exercise sovereign powers, thus symbolising the overcoming of resistance to establish sovereign rule.

Emer, the wife of CúChulainn, is also associated with edad. Although she was his true wife, she was ever jealous of his exploits with other women, chief among them being the Otherworldly woman named Fand. In the course of time, Emer was given a magical drink which made her forget her jealousies. The obvious interpretation here is that of the overcoming of such negative traits as jealousy. Celtic symbolism is usually multi-layered, however, and not so simple as it appears, and it will be apparent that jealousy itself – in certain respects – is also resonant with the E-few.

Colour:

The colour of edad is red, for it is full of fiery energy and vigour. It is the colour of the victorious battle code of this few.

Bird:

The bird associated with the E-few is the swan, which is also resonant with the G-few. The symbolism of the old tale of the "ugly duckling" can once again be used to illustrate this affinity, for the bird of the old story overcomes the resistance and mockery of its start in life to become the most beautiful bird of them all. There is a lot of teaching and wisdom stored – quite deliberately – in these old stories,

The Book of Ogham

which are descended from folklore, which is descended ultimately from magical lore. Finding the correct keys to discover and decode it, discovering the principles enshrined within, is another matter, however, and requires the adoption of the mindset of the original storytellers.

Arts and Crafts / Profession:

The profession associated with this few is that of fowling, or bird hunting. This requires a combination of stealth, cunning, patience, timing and accuracy, all of which are cognate to the meaning of the few.

Numerology:

As the nineteenth few, edad is the fourth ogham in the fourth aicme. As such, it represents a principle which can be expected to come into play in all spheres of life, throughout all dimensions of existence. This is to be expected; see below on the need for the duality of overcoming and resistance to achieve any kind of real progress, to transform living into Life.

Divinatory Meanings:

There is a dynamic polarity inherent within the E-few. On the one hand, it signifies negative or turbulent situations arising which may threaten to overwhelm the querent. On the other hand, it promises that the querent may overcome all of these challenges by drawing upon inner reserves of strength and heroism.

It is a fact that if we do not have difficult and troublesome situations in life against which to test our mettle, these inner strengths are never sought out and put into practice, and we simply stagnate, stuck in a rut. How many people do you know who fit this model, whose lives have led nowhere for years, because they have always considered it prudent to back down in the face of challenges, to take the easy route? The hero only attains a heroic state of being and is remembered through the ages because he or she is willing to fight for a vision, a purpose. In doing so, in overcoming barriers and blockages in life, they make life better for themselves and for others in terms of material success, but more importantly their spirit is empowered and enriched by the struggle. There will always be resistance to progress; the comfortable old will resist the incursions of the unknown new. Sometimes this resistance will be internal, a struggle against our own idleness or habits, sometimes it will be external as our peers insist that a new and revolutionary idea should be forgotten. It takes courage to struggle on, often alone, but to the victor the spoils.

Use of this ogham in an operative magical sense should only be done by those who are very certain that they truly want to do so. In invoking the power of overcoming, the commensurate force of resistance will likewise be invoked, and the individual will be calling a possibly traumatic but certainly transformative experience down upon him/herself. But it is indicative of edad to even dare to take this step.

The danger associated with this few, of course, is that we may become disheartened and fail. As an active force in life, this is probably the most demanding of all the oghams.

The Fifths:

Edad in Mide	Overcoming in Sovereignty	Overcoming (+)
Edad in Seis	Overcoming in Harmony	Completion (+)
Edad in Fis	Overcoming in Learning	Discipline (+)
Edad in Cath	Overcoming in Conflict	Force (+)
Edad in Blath	Overcoming in Prosperity	Craft (+)

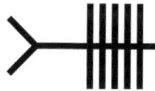

>||||

ÉO – Yew-Tree > IDAD
Death / Immortality / Transformation

Description:

Idad is a few denoting total transformation, most especially that transformation which mortals name death and fear most of all.

The Book of Ogham

The few also refers to that which is immortal within the self, however, the constant which undergoes the transformation and will survive all changes. As such, it is an ogham whose secrets may initiate grief and crisis on the surface, but which also provides great insights into the true nature of the soul for those with eyes to see them.

Word Oghams:
Word Ogham of Morainn mac Moin: Oldest tree.
Word Ogham of Maic ind Oc: Fairest of the ancients.
Word Ogham of CúChulainn: Energy of an infirm person.

As the names indicate, there is some confusion and overlap between the E-few and the I-few, but opinion seems fairly unanimous that it is this final ogham in the tale of twenty that is attributed to the yew. Due to its great age, the yew is habitually placed last in Celtic lists of trees. The first two kennings clearly point to the yew and its longevity: 'oldest tree' and 'fairest of the ancients'. The final kenning is more difficult. McManus suggests that it may be rephrased as 'sustenance of a sick person', implying the ingestion of the yew's poisoned berries, but this must remain a suggestion.

Tree:

Yew is the tree of the I-few, a tree which is much storied in all European lore. It is often found in graveyards, and is a very hardy tree, living to a very great age. It represents the paradox of life in death: the tree is an evergreen, alive when all else around it seems dead, but its fruit is poisonous, bringing death.

When the lovers Naoisi and Deirdre were buried, the Ulstermen drove yew stakes through their bodies to prevent them from being reunited in death. However, the stakes grew into two great yew trees which arched together over the cathedral at Armagh.

Deities and Heroes:

The god most clearly associated with the I-few is Lugh, through his alternate title of Ildanach. He earns this name in the tale of the "Second Battle of Magh Tured", where he lists the many skills he possesses. "Ildanach" means "many-talented", and it is a fitting

The Book of Ogham

name to be associated with the all-encompassing nature of this final ogham few. The manner in which Lugh recites his skills is also resonant with the definition of the core aspects of the soul, which is so important a feature of this few.

Also associated is Irnan, a magical hag, who challenged any member of the Fianna to fight her. She was the embodiment of great age, and weakened and subdued all who approached her. She was finally killed by the hero Goll, and this tale demonstrates the concept of the death of death itself.

Colour:

The colour attributed to the this few is "very white". This may seem peculiar to the modern mind, which automatically associates black with all things funereal. But this was not always the case, and a little thought and meditation will soon reveal the appropriateness of this attribution. The colour of death is the colour of bones bleaching in the sun, of pale, bloodless skin, but also of the clean page on which a new tale may be written.

Bird:

The eaglet is attributed to idad, a bird both noble and aloof, but also predatory, as befits the nature of this ogham.

Arts and Crafts / Profession:

The professions associated with idad are those of fishing and of woodworking in yew wood. The latter attribution is clearly related to the symbolism of the yew and its long association with burial grounds in the pagan north. The former stresses great patience and quiet.

Numerology:

The number twenty is significant as the fifth few of the fourth aicme, thus a number of cosmic importance. However, its primary emphasis derived from its placement as the final ogham in the series, as death is the final process in a life cycle.

The Book of Ogham

Divinatory Meanings:

    The primary meaning of this few is that of transformation, a total change in circumstances. The most extreme example of this type of change - and the underlying meaning of the few - is obviously that of death. In a divinatory context, however, when this ogham falls in a significant place, it will most often point to a major upheaval and/or crisis in that aspect of life to which the divination refers. This could refer to a change in job, location or personal relationships. It marks the end of one state of being and the transition to a new, different one. As such, it may infer a certain amount of discomfort and trauma if the change is unwanted or unexpected.

    In a metaphysical sense, the few does not only refer to death itself, but also to that which survives, which possesses continuity to transfer over from one state of being to the next. As such, it touches right to the core of the soul, to the root principles that make us what we are. It is a key to discovering those things within which are eternal and abiding and which may make the transition from life through death into life (see chapter 3). Used in such a manner, idad is a powerful key to self-discovery and self-actualisation.

    The main challenge of this ogham is that of overcoming the sense of loss and grief which always accompanies such traumatic change. When the old and familiar is swept irrevocably away, it can be difficult in the extreme to let it go. But until this is done, the potential of the new situation cannot be addressed and enjoyed.

The Fifths:

Idad in Mide	Death in Sovereignty	Transformation (+)
Idad in Seis	Death in Harmony	Discord (-)
Idad in Fis	Death in Learning	Disillusion (-)
Idad in Cath	Death in Conflict	Fear (-)
Idad in Blath	Death in Prosperity	Loss / Grief (-)

The Book of Ogham

Chapter 5
Layout and Casting Methods

Background

In reconstructing the actual methods used by the ancient Gaelic peoples when employing the oghams for divination, we actually have a lot of material to draw on. Through analysis of linguistic and comparative evidence, we can be fairly certain of recreating a means of ogham divination which is not only meaningful but also authentic.

It is known, for example, that the oghamic characters were carved or notched onto four-sided, elongated staves, called crann-chur in Old Irish and coelbren in Welsh, and that these staves were used in divinatory rites.

It is also a fact that all of the Indo-European peoples used some form of lot-casting as a means of divination. The Germanic folk cast their runestaves and the Romans had their sortilege. These two peoples were those most closely akin to the Celts, so they are the best sources for any comparative evidence.

The most important items to know when reconstructing a particular culture's divinatory rites, however, are the matters we have discussed in the preceding chapters, namely their cosmology and the analytical system in which they have encoded the keys to understanding the universe and its functions (i.e. in the case of the

145

Celts, the ogham fews.) The cosmology provides a mental map of the world, ordered in the way most meaningful to the psyche of the diviner, and the analytical system provides a secret metalanguage of this world. When the symbols of this metalanguage are laid over the symbolic cosmic map in a ritualised setting, reliable and consistent synchronicities can be expected to result, which are harmonious with the world view expressed by the system involved. This is the way in which almost all systems of divination work. For example, in astrology the constellations are juxtaposed to symbolic houses, and planets are juxtaposed to the constellations and houses. With the tarot, cards are laid over a pattern where each position where a card is laid has a predetermined significance, according to which the card is interpreted. With the runes, the staves are cast upon steads of meaning. And so forth.

The oghams represent the Celtic analytical view of the world. This remains a truth even if you choose to deny the more mystical elements of life and treat the ogham primarily as an aid to memorisation and a poetic tool. It is ultimately an attempt to codify and classify all of existence in a meaningful way. We have already investigated the reconstruction of the Celtic cosmological map, which provides that pattern upon which the ogham characters can be cast for the purpose of divination. Having recovered these two essential keys, we can now rediscover a true system of ogham divination.

Working Methods

Contrary to popular belief, divination with the ogham fews is not a parlour game. It is a sacred act, to be carried out with proper respect and dignity. There is a world of difference between ogham divination and party time fortune-telling. This chapter will help prepare you and your tools for correctly interfacing with the divine (which is what the word "divination" actually means).

The Book of Ogham

Making and Charging the Cloth

Divination should be carried out in a sacred space. In ogham divination, this is represented by casting or placing the fews upon a prepared surface: either a cloth or a wooden surface. If a cloth, it should be either pure white (representing clarity of vision); deep green (representing the Otherworld); or pure black (representing the hidden mysteries to be discovered). If a wooden surface is used, it should ideally be birch (the first wood in the ogham series); rowan (traditionally associated with divination); oak (sacred to the druids); or yew (representing the wisdom of ages).

The surface should be about three feet square and be divided into sections as shown in figure 5.1. If a cloth is used, these can be drawn on with permanent inks, or embroidered. If a wooden surface is employed, the pattern can be carved upon it, then coloured if necessary. The colour(s) used may be chosen at the discretion of the diviner, but green or blue would be appropriate in all circumstances.

In all cases, the cloth or board should be magically charged as follows before actually being used for divinatory purposes.

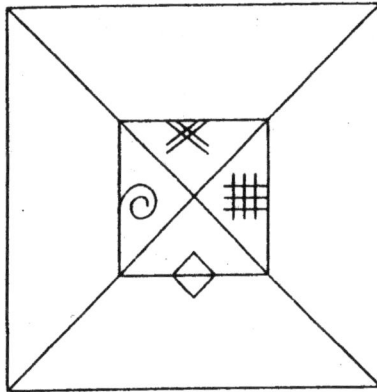

Figure 5.1 The pattern of the casting cloth or board

The Book of Ogham

When the cloth has been prepared, lay it before you, facing north, and recite the following invocation. This will align the symbolic pattern on the cloth with the forces at work in the world around you:

> Before me stands Ériu in Fal,
> on my right stands Nuada in Gor,
> on my left stands the Dagda in Mur,
> and at my back stands Lugh in Fin.
> May each bless me and go before me in all that I do
> here.

As you recite this, visualise the four towering forms surrounding you at the cardinal points of the cosmos, focusing their power toward you. The one in the north will be standing upon a stone, the one to the right will be holding a spear, the one to the left will be standing behind a cauldron, and the one behind you will be holding a sword.

Then call upon the ancestral gods and goddesses of the Celts to assist you in your work and to lay their blessing and power upon the cloth:

> I call upon all the Gods and Goddesses on which my
> forebears called and swore their oaths. Come, be with
> me in all I do here. I call upon the Dagda, the Good
> God; upon Lugh, the Shining One; upon the strong
> Ogma; and upon Manannán of the Deep.

Once you have consecrated the cloth or board in this manner, it should not be allowed to be trivialised. It is now a sacred object, and should be treated as such.

Making and Charging the Ogham Fews

We know that the ogham fews were traditionally carved upon squared-off strips of wood. Lengths of hardwood about quarter of an inch square can be obtained from most craft or hardware shops, and can be cut into lengths of about three or four inches. The feather mark should be cut into the bottom of the few, and the notches should be carved along the same edge, either to the left or right of the edge as appropriate. An example of the few for straif is shown in figure 5.2.

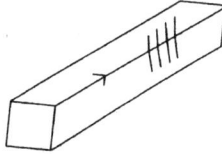

Figure 5.2 Example of the straif few

In an ideal world, each few would be carved from the actual wood associated with that ogham (the straif example shown above would be carved on blackthorn, for instance). This ideal state of affairs is certainly something to ultimately aspire to, but you should not delay working with the oghams until you are able to find samples of all the various woods. By all means work at crafting a "perfect" set of oghams as a long-term project, but first make a basic working set to use in the meantime. Initially, carve your set of oghams from a single type of wood, for simplicity's sake. Any of the following three options will serve you well in practice while you work towards perfection:

1. You may decide upon using a single wood of a meaningful nature. Good choices would be birch, as first in the ogham series and the first recorded wood to be used in oghamic magic; or oak, because of its close association with the druids.
2. For the sake of convenience, and to enable you to get to work with the oghams as quickly as possible (very important), you may use a basic hardwood from a craft shop.
3. Even paper and card are derived from trees, and a set of ogham carefully drawn upon card and consecrated will serve you well in the early stages.

Whichever option you choose, do not fall into the trap of delaying work until you can "do better". Do the best you can now, and aspire to better later. This is a good rule for life in general

The ritual of making the fews is as follows. Gather together

The Book of Ogham

your tools (the strips of wood, a knife to carve them with, and red ink or paint). An open flame (a candle will be sufficient) should be on your right and an open container of water on your left. Sit or stand facing north. Then invoke the directional forces:

Before me stands Ériu in Fal,
on my right stands Nuada in Gor,
on my left stands the Dagda in Mur,
and at my back stands Lugh in Fin.
May each bless me and go before me in all that I do here.

As you recite this, visualise the four towering forms surrounding you at the cardinal points of the cosmos, focusing their power toward you. The one in the north will be standing upon a stone, the one to the right will be holding a spear, the one to the left will be standing behind a cauldron, and the one behind you will be holding a sword.

Then call upon the ancestral gods and goddesses of the Celts to assist you in your work and to lay their blessing and power upon it:

I call upon all the Gods and Goddesses on which my forebears called and swore their oaths. Come, be with me in all I do here. I call upon the Dagda, the Good God; upon Lugh, the Shining One; upon the strong Ogma; and upon Manannán of the Deep.

Then speak the following invocation before actually commencing the carving of the fews:

I call upon you, the three Brigids, to guide my hands and the ogham fews. I call upon you, the three Morríghna, to guide my hand that I may make the fews good and true.

Then begin carving the ogham fews, taking each in turn and

150

in its proper order, commencing with beithe and ending with idad. Carve the feather mark and the notches, then use the red ink to colour the feather, the notches, and the edge along which they are carved. As you do so, you may wish to focus your mind upon the meaning of the few, and whisper or "sing" its name into the wood. Then set it aside to dry and take up the next few for carving and colouring.

To dedicate the fews for use, take each one in your hand and silently think its name while you sprinkle it with water and pass it through the flame. This process may be repeated periodically in order to clear from the fews any undesirable influences that may have accreted to them.

Once prepared and consecrated, the fews should be carefully stored in a cloth or leather bag used exclusively for the purpose. Like the casting cloth, your ogham fews are sacred objects and should be treated as such.

The Ritual of Reading the Oghams

It is not necessary to go to great ritual lengths when reading the oghams, and the degree of formal structuring employed can be quite comfortably varied according to the desires of the reader. The following stages are suggested as a workable formula, however, and each of these should really be addressed by the diviner, however briefly:

1. Lay out the casting cloth to the north of your position. This provides the sacred space for the reading.
2. An opening invocation or gesture(s).
3. Invocation of the ancestral gods and goddesses who give insight.
4. Call for the guidance of the Morríghna and/or Brigid in the operation.
5. Do the actual layout or casting.
6. Focus attention by means of a magical gesture.
7. Interpret the reading in a focused and insightful state of mind.

151

The Book of Ogham

The following example is suggested as being straightforward and authentically Celtic.

1.   Define the Sacred Space.

Face north and lay out the casting cloth before you, with the bag containing the oghams alongside it.

2.   The Opening.

Hold your arms straight out at your sides, assuming a cross-like posture, and say:

> Before me stands Ériu in Fal,
> on my right stands Nuada in Gor,
> on my left stands the Dagda in Mur,
> and at my back stands Lugh in Fin.
> May each bless me and go before me in all that I do
> here.

As you recite this, visualise the four towering forms surrounding you at the cardinal points of the cosmos, focusing their power toward you. The one in the north will be standing upon a stone, the one to the right will be holding a spear, the one to the left will be standing behind a cauldron, and the one behind you will be holding a sword.

3.   The Invocation.

Still facing north, hold your arms straight out before you and say:

> I call upon all the Gods and Goddesses on which my
> forebears called and swore their oaths. Come, be with
> me in all I do here. I call upon the Dagda, the Good
> God; upon Lugh, the Shining One; upon the strong
> Ogma; and upon Manannán of the Deep.

152

The Book of Ogham

4.   The Call.

Take your position before the casting cloth, where you will actually
cast the fews. Hold your hands with palms upward just below your
mouth and say over them:

>   I call upon you, the three Brigids, to guide my hands
>   and the ogham fews. I call upon you, the three
>   Morríghna, to guide my mind and the ogham fews that
>   I might see and read in them what is right and true.

5.   The Layout or Casting.

Now take the ogham fews out of their bag and lay or cast them upon
the cloth in the predetermined pattern of the method of reading you
are using. Once they are all in their places, proceed to the ritual
gesture.

6.   The Gesture.

The ritual gesture is intended to focus the mind and direct it upon the
task of interpretation, entering a state of consciousness where the
subtle relationships between the symbols may be correctly perceived
and remarked upon. This gesture may be personally conceived, but a
couple of traditional suggestions would be as follows: (1) place the
right palm over the left eye and the left palm over the right eye. This
symbolises the withdrawal of the mind's attention from the realm of
the mundane senses into a more reflective state; (2) more suited to
some personalities would be to bite upon the thumb to the point of
causing pain, thus sharpening and focusing the mind in the realm of
the senses, but making it more alert than normal.

7.   The Reading.

You should now begin the process of interpreting the reading in
accordance with the pattern / method you have chosen. Whether you

The Book of Ogham

are doing the reading for yourself or for another, it is always helpful to speak your insights out loud. Doing so compels you to shape thoughts into words, giving them more "substance" and meaning. You may wish to make a tape recording of the spoken reading for future reference. At the very least, you should record the details of the reading and layout on paper so that it may be referred to again. As time passes and you gain experience with the oghams, you may find that they begin to speak to you in unique ways, communicating specific ideas to you. You stand a better chance of discovering and making active use of such tendencies if you are able to periodically review previous readings with the benefit of hindsight.

Methods of Reading Oghams

Four different methods of reading the oghams are suggested here. Initially, you should familiarise yourself with all four, trying them out. Having done so, you may wish to specialise in the one which seems to speak to you most clearly at this time. Having become an expert in that style of reading, you can then move on to increased mastery of the others. They each have their own emphasis and signification, but ultimately they all serve to provide a means whereby the soul may communicate with the hidden realms. Having mastered all four, you may like to experiment further with the alternate methods of drawing fews or superimposing multiple layers of readings as suggested at the end of this chapter.

1. The Way of Brigid

This is the simplest of the methods of reading the oghams presented here. It is based upon the cosmological significance of the number three to the Celts, with the model of this world (bith) with the Underworld beneath it and the Otherworld over it. It also echoes the triple aspect of certain of the Celtic gods and goddesses, such as Brigid and Lugh. The interplay of these three realms is symbolised by the

154

threefold spiral of the triskelion (figure 5.3), which is a particularly Celtic symbol (as witness the "three legs" version of the triskelion which is the national flag of the Isle of Man). It pictures perfectly the dynamic interchange between the three Celtic levels of existence.

Figure 5.3 The Triskelion

It is this interplay of realms which this method of reading seeks to uncover and render sensible. It should uncover the roots of a question and examine its implications and the manner of its unfolding in all levels of reality.

Three fews should be drawn and placed one above the other, as indicated in figure 5.4.

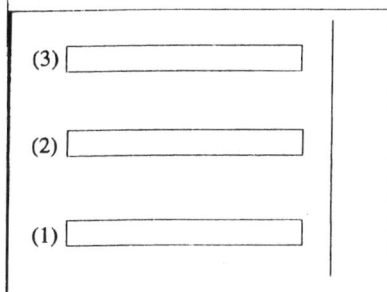

Figure 5.4 The Layout of Brigid

The lowermost of the three fews represents the Underworld, where the root of the matter lies. It is here that you will find the hidden influences from which the situation in question has been born. It may also deal with those aspects of life often colloquially described

The Book of Ogham

as being "earthy", such as matters relating to wealth or the erotic. It may also represent the past – possibly even previous existences in extreme cases – and those dark, hidden causes which escape our conscious notice.

The middle few represents this world of three dimensions – bith. As such, it represents the situation as it stands now, the position in which you find yourself, and/or the manner in which that position affects you and helps or hinders the question. This few should be read with specific reference to the way in which it emerges from the Underworld roots. The way in which this mortal world manifests from the Underworld may give some clue as to what action needs to be taken to set a troubled situation back on its proper course.

The final, uppermost few represents the Otherworld. this cannot truly be said to represent the future as such, for the Otherworld experiences the flow of time in ways far different from our own accustomed three-dimensional world. It ebbs and flows, and contains all possibilities within itself. Nevertheless, the few in this position can generally be taken to foreshadow the probable outcome of the situation in question. It will surely prefigure those opportunities which the querent should be made aware of, and may open the eyes to meaningful synchronicities which would otherwise be missed. If viewed with an open mind instead of being shoehorned into a rigid world view, the few in this position can provide great guidance. (Macbeth's misinterpretations of the Weird Sisters' prophecies based upon his own rigid expectations is a good example of how not to interpret Otherworldly guidance.)

It will be found with practice that this is the method of ogham divination which is open to the greatest extent of subjective interpretation and intuition. It presents the least quantity of objective symbolism (a mere three fews in three steads) to the diviner, and yet this is often sufficient for readings of remarkable depth and accuracy. This method favours those who already possess some degree of psychic ability, but will assist all who persist with it to develop such ability, even if it currently lies dormant.

The Book of Ogham

Sample Reading in the Way of Brigid

Question: Should I commit my funds to attending a convention so that I can teach what I have learned?

Note: The subject had recently uncovered some new understandings and insight which had turned his own life around. He felt a tremendous need to travel to attend an esoteric conference overseas in order to share what he had learned on a face to face basis. This would have obvious advantages in terms of receiving feedback and in terms of developing his ideas. At the present, however, his financial position was precarious and this journey would use all of his money. He would be faced with a few months of hard financial balancing upon his return.

The layout is done and the position of the fews is recorded.

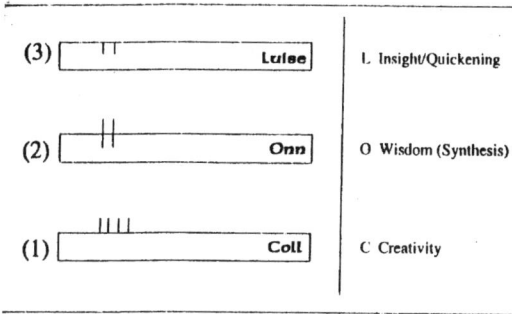

(3)	Luise	L Insight/Quickening
(2)	Onn	O Wisdom (Synthesis)
(1)	Coll	C Creativity

Figure 5.5 Sample Reading in the Way of Brigid

Records of layouts done by this method do not need to be any more complicated than the diagram shown in figure 5.5. Simply inscribing the Roman letters corresponding to the three fews in the proper order does quite nicely. Under each letter, you can make a listing of the data relevant to the reading and maintain a permanent yet flexible record of the interpretation.

157

The Book of Ogham

Reading: The roots of the question lie in the subject's creative mind, and the inspiration for his work (C). This explains quite well the strength of the subject's driving need to sacrifice his short term material comfort in order to attend this esoteric conference.

The position in this world signifies that the subject has obtained wisdom of great worth from his endeavours (O). It is this which he now wishes to share with his peers in order to benefit further from their insightful feedback. In this way he hopes to attain further wisdom. The subject is a great believer in the practice of teaching by the mouth to ear method of direct personal interaction.

The few of the Otherworld is extremely propitious for the querent's purpose, promising further insights and greater awakening if he follows his plan through (L). True to the nature of this few, the subject is enlivened by this reading and immediately begins making arrangements for his journey.

2. The Way of the Fifths

We have already explored the significance of the fivefold model of reality to the Celts in chapter 2. This method of divination uses this symbolic map of the cosmos to examine the forces at play in the querent's life and world at the time the question is asked. The model used by the Celts was that of a cross-shaped figure: a central field, surrounded by four other fields or planes. Perhaps the importance of this cross-shaped symbol to the pre-Christian Celts explains the huge number of carved crosses (often equilateral, similar to the model here) attributed to the early Celtic church.

This method of reading examines the querent in relation to the forces moving into manifestation through the fifths of the cosmos. The querent can be pictured as standing in the centre of his world, caught in the middle of a cross-flow of forces. This reading reveals those forces acting upon the querent's life.

If the Way of Brigid is the most subjective of the reading methods presented here, the Way of the Fifths is probably the most objective, relying heavily upon the meanings defined in the tables of interpretations listed under each of the fews in chapter 4. Five fews should be drawn randomly and laid upon the casting cloth in the order numbered in figure 5.6.

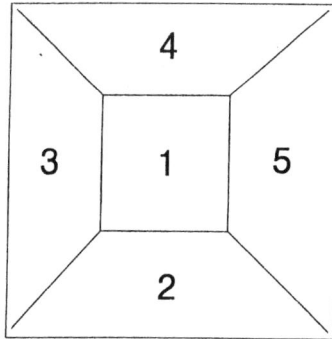

Figure 5.6 The Layout of the Fifths

The easiest way to begin a reading in the Way of the Fifths is to quickly list the meanings of the fews in their positions as determined from the tables on interpretation in chapter 4. This is only the beginning, however, as many subtle currents and shades of meaning run through this layout to the experienced eye.

The fifths are symbolised in the ogham by the forfedha. n their turn, the fifths may help us to understand these mysterious additional symbols. Fews cast or laid in the fifths, each of which is governed by a forfidh, are to be read and understood within the meaning of that symbol according to the following keys:

⟩✕ (ea) – Mide / Rige: This is the central position of the reading, and thus the central focus of the question. It is appropriate that it is the cosmological position of the centre of the world, namely the individual consciousness. When analysing a reading, all will be referred back to this point. When a reading is done on behalf of more than one person, such as a couple, a family, or an organisation, this represents a form of "collective identity" for the purpose of the reading.

The Book of Ogham

>◇ (oi) - Seis: This represents the influences upon the situation from the remote past.

>☞ (ui) - Fis: This shows the influences which have most recently been developing with regard to the question. It shows the influence of the more recent past.

>✖ (io) - Cath: This represents those influences which will arise in the near future to provide resistance to the querent's wishes. These are the obstacles to be overcome. Of course, if fews indicative of great strength for the querent arise in this position, it may indicate that there is little or no resistance and that what little there is will be swiftly overcome.

>☰ (ae) - Blath: This represents the force of manifestation, of things coming into being through the influence of crossing currents of force. As such, it represents the outcome of the question, the result which will most likely be made manifest. This should be referred back to the subject of the question in the Mide position to reveal its true meaning.

Begin the reading by starting at the central position and then reading around the spiral of the other fews in numeric order, from Seis to Blath. Having assessed this initial spiral unfolding of the reading, see if you can gain any further insights by considering the cross currents implicit in the layout. Assess the combined meanings of the fews in positions 2 and 4 in relation to the subject, and then likewise assess the combined meanings of the fews in positions 3 and 5. When the impact of both the spiral unfoldment of the question and the cross currents upon the subject have been revealed, you will have a great deal of insight into the question. If the final meaning or guidance remains uncertain, it is permissible at this stage to lay one further few upon the central position to symbolise a summation of all these influences upon the subject. This may assist to wrap the reading up successfully. Do be aware, however, that some readings may have indeterminate outcomes; in such cases, an examination of the fews in the layout will often show that the subject him/herself does not really know what he/she wants. In such a case, the guidance should be to make a decision before proceeding; the deciding factors lie within, not

160

without.

Sample Reading in the Way of the Fifths

Question: What will be the outcome of the changes I am now making in my life?

Note: The subject was a woman who had decided to uproot and return to her home town of several years earlier. She was concerned to know how disruptive or unsettling this major move would be, and whether she would be readily accepted back into her old community.

The layout is done and the positions of the fews are recorded. Records of layouts done by this method need not be any more complex than the diagram shown in figure 5.7. Simply inscribing the Roman letter for the few in the proper fifth is quite sufficient.

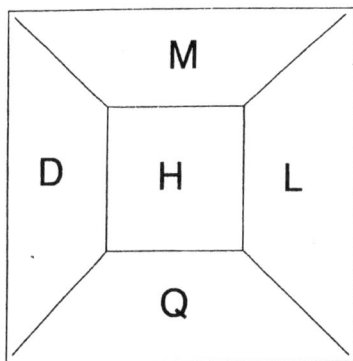

Figure 5.7 Sample Reading in the Way of the Fifths

Reading: The H-few in the central position indicates weakness and is a good indicator of the subject's fears and apprehensions in the face of the planned life upheaval. The hawthorn represents the period of waiting before Mayday. This reading was carried out in the month of

The Book of Ogham

May, and given the emphasis of the rest of the reading, I told the subject her fears and concerns would be gone before the end of the month, that this period of apprehension was drawing to a swift end.

The Q-few indicates satisfaction. It is a harmonious few in the place of harmony. Looking to the past, it shows the happy times the subject had in her former home, a place she always found to be peaceful and beautiful.

The D-few in the place of learning means recognition. The subject should know that she had friends in her old community and they have not forgotten her. In spite of her worries, she will be welcomed back.

The M-few in the place of conflict implies pride. The subject has nothing to fear, nobody is going to put any obstacles in her path. Indeed, I told her that I had an absolute conviction that her path would be so easy and straightforward that it would be almost too good to be true.

The L-few in the place of prosperity puts the cap on an extraordinarily positive reading. The outcome will be one of abundance. Nothing can go wrong here.

Postscript: Only two days after this reading, I received a phone call. The subject had met with her old friends, had been accepted by them and had not been made to feel a stranger; she was treated as if she had never been away. Furthermore, she had made an offer for a well-priced flat with a fantastic view and her offer had been accepted already. This confirmed the reading's emphasis of a rapid resolution to her fears, and a quick and painless reintegration into the community.

3. The Way of Casting on the Fifths

The cosmological lore necessary to the interpretation of the Way of Casting on the Fifths is identical to that employed for the standard Way of the Fifths reading method described above. It revolves around an interpretation of the ogham fews as they fall within the spaces of the four cosmic directions and the centre. This type of

The Book of Ogham

"casting" reading is carried out in a very different way to the other methods presented here, however, employing greater randomness. It affords an extremely thorough reading, offering a great deal of objective data, but also demands a high degree of subjective interpretation and analysis of the "weighting" of the reading. It provides a lengthy and involved reading, but can throw considerable light on complicated or multi-layered questions.

Instead of laying selected fews in predefined positions on the casting cloth, the diviner stands over it and draws the fews out of their bag and literally scatters them randomly over the cloth, letting them lie where they fall. This should be done without looking. The process of casting the fews allows for an enormous amount of variables in a reading. In theory, they might be scattered evenly throughout the five fields, or all twenty fews might conceivably fall within a single field. Some may even miss the casting cloth altogether and thus be noticeable by their absence in the reading. The scattering provides valuable clues to the reader as to the weighting and emphasis of the reading.

Initially, read the fews in the same way as in the Way of the Fifths, according a meaning to each few corresponding to the field it lies in. An overall picture of the blended meanings of the fews in each fifth should gradually emerge. Some fews will reinforce the influence of others, and still others will provide caveats and words of warning. A meaningful synthesis of the overall reading should thus arise.

Then begin exploring the details. Which fews run parallel to each other, or which cross each other, thus supporting or resisting each others' influence? What fews lie along or across the boundaries between fields, and what effect does this have upon their influence? Which fews are conspicuous by their absence, having fallen outside the area of the casting cloth? These subtle symbolic signs should now be sought and interpreted by the diviner. There is tremendous scope for subjective insights to rise to the fore here, especially as your experience grows and as the oghams become a living, flowing force within your own being. You will become able to discern patterns in the casting which speak loudly to you in time.

With this method of reading, it is absolutely essential to keep

The Book of Ogham

an accurate record. You must copy down the exact position of each few, the angle on which it lies and the direction in which it points. No other method will enable you to recapture the subtleties of the reading at a later date should you wish to review it.

Sample Reading in the Way of Casting on the Fifths

Question: Is it wise to try to find a partner through internet contact ads?

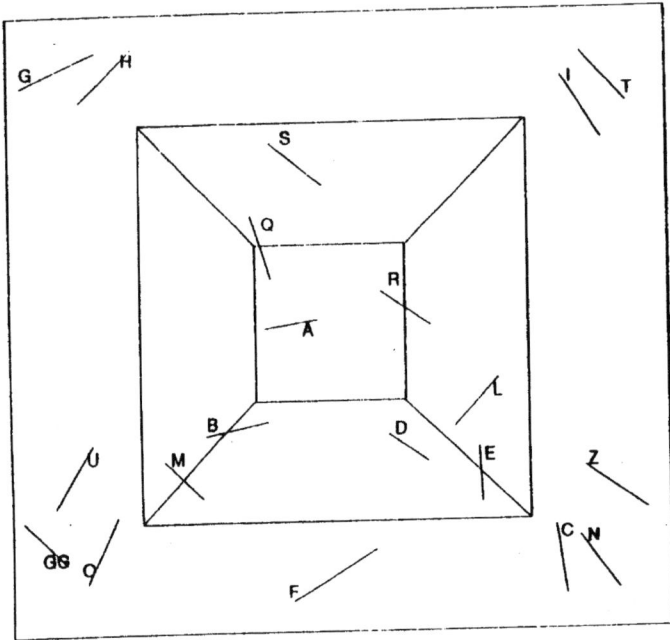

Figure 5.8 Sample Reading of the Way of Casting on the Fifths

Note: The subject had been looking for a romantic liaison for several months. On the spur of the moment, he had replied to a contact ad

164

The Book of Ogham

on the internet, seeing this as a yet unexplored avenue. Although the deed was already done, he consulted with the diviner to ascertain its wisdom and potential.

The Reading: The first two things to be noted in this reading are (1) that it is a very dynamic reading, as so many of the fews have fallen in positions where they cross from one field into another, thus shifting their influence, and (2) the large number of fews which fell outside of the casting area (the outermost area in figure 5.8). In this latter respect, it is interesting to take note from the outset that both of the fews usually considered most "unfortunate" in divination – úath and straith – have no influence upon the reading. It is initially more surprising to note that ur is also missing, as both of its meanings, as a gateway and as passion, would seem relevant to the question. However, some reflection suggested that the subject had already used the gateway before consulting the diviner, and passion would only be likely to occur at a later stage if the querent's approach internet usage proved successful. This reminded me at the time that the purpose of the reading was to determine the wisdom and potential of an action the querent had already taken.

Moving on to examine the fields in the reading, it is immediately apparent that the subject's Sovereignty (A) is firmly centered in himself, which would suggest that the process he has begun reflects something which is essential to him and not just a romantic folly. Although he sees the internet as a perfect tool in his cause, he is not without his doubts, hence the need for this reading (this interpretation is based upon the influence of the Q-few passing from Mide into Cath). He is now giving serious thought to the question of a new long-term relationship, and has acquired a world view and a station in life which gives him something to genuinely offer a potential mate (the R-few, passing from Mide into Blath).

Over the past several months, the subject has experienced increasing discontent with his aloneness (D), and has now behaved slightly uncharacteristically and has taken steps to change his situation in a new way (the B-few, passing from Seis into Fis). The disturbance this brings to his outlook is not unwelcome, however, indeed he

165

relishes it. He is perhaps overly modest in general (M), and this new approach helps to step around that problem. Indeed, his desire for success in this question pushes him to use all means at his disposal in order to get a result, the internet included (the E-few, passing from Seis into Blath).

His intuitive faculties (S) will give him an advantage over all obstacles which may appear in his path. He should trust his feelings and go with his inner convictions.

The final result is one of abundance (L). Despite the subject's retrospective reservations about his impulsive action, this should be a method which will work for him, a very successful and life-changing step.

Postscript: The subject's reply to the ad was met with a very favourable response. At the time of writing, the relationship is still ongoing and developing well.

4. The Way of the Worlds

One of the most famous tarot card layouts is that colloquially called the "Celtic Cross". Probably quite unconsciously, this description is not so inaccurate, as that spread depicts the expanded (or rather, unfolded) pattern of the Celtic fifths. On that basis, a variant of the layout is presented here for use with the ogham. It seems inaccurate to lay the final four fews in a line to the right of the reading, as is generally done with the tarot cards. Instead, they will be laid in their appropriate positions within the fields of Celtic cosmology, providing another turn of the spiral of manifestation out from the centre. In this way, the true interrelationship between the fews in the reading can be seen, and the crosswise currents described in the Way of the Fifths can be even more readily discerned. This reading method should provide a little familiar ground and be a good "crossover" one for someone who is accustomed to reading the tarot and now wishes to learn ogham.

It should be noted that although this is intended to be a method for laying the fews, it can if desired also be used as a pattern for casting the fews upon, following the same general guidelines as for the Way of Casting on the Fifths, given above. Personally, I find this overcomplicates matters and gets in the way of the subjective patterns which can be discerned when the fifths alone are used. This is only my personal preference, however, and you should probably try casting on the ninefold pattern at least once; it may suit you.

The fews should be laid out in the order and pattern shown in figure 5.9.

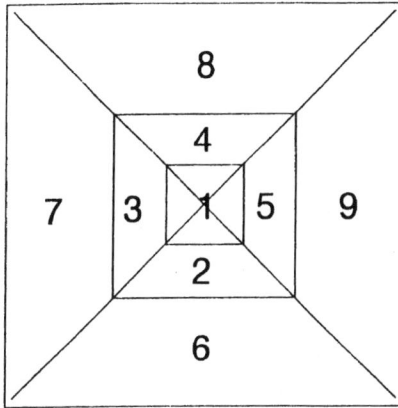

Figure 5.9 The Pattern of the Ninefold Layout

The positions should be interpreted according to the following keys:

1. This indicates the present state or the self of the subject.
2. This provides background information which bears upon the matter in question in relation to the subject. This position relates to those things which already lie within the experience of the subject.
3. This indicates influences which are just passing away.
4. This indicates an influence towards which the subject is heading which will have some bearing upon the question. Note that this influence is always dependent upon the subject and his/her current

direction. It may therefore be avoided.
5. This also represents an influence which looms upon the near horizon, but its emphasis is different. This is an influence which will arise with regard to the matter in question which will have some bearing on the subject and his relations with it.
6. This position reveals the fears and anxieties of the subject in relation to the situation.
7. This indicates the social environment in which the subject is placed, and its influence upon the question (and vice versa).
8. Here the subject's hopes and ideals relating to the situation.
9. Here we find the final outcome.

As a rule of thumb, the "inner ring", comprising fields 2 to 5, can be said to reflect the inner, subjective state of the subject relating to the question, while the "outer ring" of fields 6 to 9 reflects the outer, objective matters relating to the question.

When reading using this method, there are several weightings and patterns which should be taken into account:

1. Read the unfolding spiral of the layout in numeric order first.
2. Pay attention to the pairs of fews located in each fifth (i.e. positions 2/6, 3/7, etc.) Decide how they each modify one another's meaning, and how their meanings are combined in their influence upon the subject.
3. As in the Way of the Fifths, analyse the effects of the crossed patterns of force, both against each other and upon the subject (e.g. 2/6 balanced and contrasted against 4/8, and the effects of all of these upon 1). It will be observed that there are many polarities to be investigated and balanced in this style of reading, such as the balance between the subject's fears and hopes in positions 6 and 8 respectively.

Sample Reading in the Way of the Worlds

Question: The querent has always been on friendly terms with Ms X.

The Book of Ogham

Has he been wrong to dismiss the idea of a more romantic relationship with her out of hand?

Note: The subject was actively looking for a partner, and in a previous reading had been advised to keep his eyes open to all possibilities instead of becoming obsessively focused on one or two options only. He ran the danger of not seeing the forest for the trees. (Incidentally, this querent is a different person from the one in the previous example reading. You will quickly learn that the questions most often asked are those relating to either love or money, in a ratio of about 3:2.)

He now returned for a follow up reading as he was concerned that he might have been too dismissive of a single woman with whom he had been friends for a long time. He had never considered her as a potential partner and now wondered what the potential might be.

One complication was that the subject strongly desired to start a family and have children, but Ms X was incapable of childbearing.

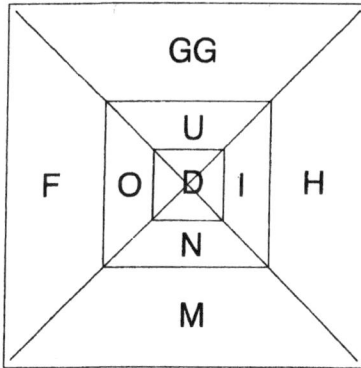

Figure 5.10 Sample Reading in the Ninefold Method

The Reading: The D-few indicates that the subject is in a strong position, and he is commended for heeding the previous reading and

169

keeping his eyes open to all possibilities. He has realised that one such has been right under his nose for a long time but has never been given proper consideration before. However, the N-few is not well placed in Seis, the implication being that this relationship could be as much a trap as anything; it would disrupt the subject's life and other plans to a degree he might not be able to cope with.

The depth of the friendship between these two people is shown by the O-few with its pleasant and harmonious implications, and the potential for genuine passion is shown on the horizon. The indications are that if the subject decided to push for a more intimate relationship with Ms X, she would certainly reciprocate, and many of the right ingredients would be present for both of them. However, the presence of the I-few foreshadows a sense of loss if this should go ahead.

The subject's fears illuminate this, as he is apprehensive about the merging of personal worlds with this person, which any successful relationship would require. This does not imply any fault with their long and well-founded friendship, it simply implies that the transformation of this friendship into a romance would not be something that the subject really wants. His hopes are for a harmonious and pleasing relationship, but these must be weighed against his fears of becoming enmeshed in a deeper relationship with Ms X.

The H-few as a final outcome, reinforced by the I-few, is absolutely adamant that this relationship would be a bad idea. But this is not to be taken as critical of the deep and fruitful friendship the two have. Given their suitability in so many other ways, and the subject's stated desire to have children, it becomes clear that her inability to bear him a family would be a real problem to him, which would prove too great an obstacle for the relationship to survive. The reading is quite clear that their friendship is too good to spoil by pushing it into something he does not want it to be.

Note: care must always be taken when interpreting and balancing such emotionally charged readings as the above. It quickly becomes apparent that the querent does not actually want a romantic relationship with Ms X. Nor has she ever dropped hints that she wants such a relationship with him. Although, given the depth of their friendship, such a relationship could work, it is obvious from the reading that it would be ultimately unhappy and unfulfilling for both of them. It is important to stress the continuation of the friendship at the same time as downplaying the relationship idea. Answers to most questions, even ones which seem simple on the surface, will be multifaceted, and with practice you will get the balance right. The above reading would have been rendered much more complex had Ms X actually been making it obvious that she wanted a romantic entanglement with the subject; fortunately, such was not the case. Keep your mind alert for all the subtly different layers of a reading.

The layout methods and sample readings provided should assist you in trying your own hand at ogham divination. Take it one step at a time, look for the obvious, and gradually the ogham fews will open many different subtle streams of insights to your senses. Those who choose to practise the suggested curriculum of study in this book will find that ogham becomes a part of their way of thinking much more quickly, a living inner stream of knowledge and wisdom upon which they can draw, of which the outer fews are merely symbolic.

Alternate Ways of Drawing Fews

In all of the layout methods described above, it is only possible to lay each particular ogham few in a single place in a given reading. In actual fact, however, the influence of that few might extend into more than one area of a situation, and it might be expected to show itself in more than one position in a reading.

You may therefore like to experiment with a couple of alternate methods of drawing fews. (These will obviously only be workable with the methods which involve laying the fews in predetermined positions; the method of casting the fews cannot really be amended.) The first of these methods simply allows for the possibility of a given few occurring in more than one place in a reading. The second method involves laying out the fews more than once and synthesising their meanings.

171

The Book of Ogham

Instead of laying out each few in turn, one after the other, instead draw a single few from the bag and lay it in the first position. Note this few in that position on a piece of paper which will record the layout. The few is then returned to the bag and another few is drawn out. This few is marked in the second position on the piece of paper. In theory this second few could be the same as the first one. It is then returned to the bag and another is drawn for the third position, and so on until the layout is completed. The reading is then made as normal from the written record of the layout, the only difference being that certain fews may recur.

I have found it remarkably effective and informative to lay three "layers" of fews for an in-depth reading. First, lay the fews on the casting cloth as normal, and note their positions. Then collect them up and return them to the bag. Now lay out a fresh set of fews on the positions. These should be noted alongside the first set. These too are returned to the bag and a third set of fews are laid out and noted. This gives a total of three fews in each position, and is a highly accurate and subtle method of reading for those experienced in interpreting the influence of several fews all modifying each other. It is a very rich and informative style of reading, and the incidence of recurrence of the same few in the same or supportive places can be remarkable. It adds considerable depth and emphasis to a reading.

Prophecy: An Advanced Technique of Divination

One of the magical / divinatory arts extensively practised by the druids and bards was that of prophecy. In popular terminology, prophecy is generally taken to be a means of foretelling the future. It can indeed encompass this as part of its function, but it is actually an art with a much broader purpose.

Basically, prophecy can probably be best described as an "inspired utterance", i.e. a message in words which has its origins in supra-rational realms, a message from gods to men, from the hidden inner world to the outer world. This message may be a warning of imminent error or danger, it may be an encouragement, it may reveal

172

The Book of Ogham

all manner of arcane mysteries. Prophecies, probably due to their origins in the deepest, most archetypal part of the psyche, are often deeply symbolic. A good historical example is the Prophecy of Merlin, recorded at great length in Geoffrey of Monmouth's Histories of the Kings of Britain.

One obvious question is whether prophecy has an extra-human source? Is it indeed a direct communication from gods to men, or is it a welling up of insights and perceptions from the innermost recesses of the human soul? I believe it can be both. The psyche, awakened by prolonged practice with the ogham and experience of the currents of the fews as they manifest in life, may discern many things which are not immediately apparent to the conscious mind. These may include the broad pattern of events which are shaping the present, and thus afford hints to the possible future. It may include subtle fragments of information which the intuition can weave into a much larger picture. All of these deep level perceptions, which normally go unnoticed, can and do come through in the act of prophecy. Similarly, the ancestral gods and goddesses may communicate directly within the deepest recesses of the human mind and inspire a prophecy which purports to afford a unique and direct understanding of the purposes of the gods. Such latter type of prophecies, it must be stressed, are certainly the exception rather than the rule and should never be simply accepted at face value.

Of course, all of the flaws and prejudices of the human personality also shape and "flavour" the message which is delivered through that personality, whether the source of that message lies within or without. Personal bias, wish fulfillment, previous indoctrination – all of these factors have a bearing. This should always be borne in mind, whether examining your own prophetic utterances or those offered by others; the messenger is indeed a good indicator of the value of the message. The greater the integrity and sensitivity of the prophet, the more sure we can be that the message as delivered remains close to its true source meaning. It is not enough to prophesy; your prophecies must stand up to scrutiny. Only the most advanced and lucid souls can expect to be a direct spokesperson for the gods. The practice of prophecy for personal illumination and insight, however, is most useful and an art worth persevering with.

When Merlin prophesied, he either burst into tears or roared with wild, uncontrollable laughter. Prophecy is triggered by an emotional dam burst, which opens the channels between the deep places of the psyche and the more familiar parts, allowing an exchange to occur. Let's take an example: a woman skilled in Celtic lore faces a dilemma. She does not know whether to remain in her current well-paid job, where the future prospects are good, or whether to uproot and move to another country where she has always wanted to live. She deliberately sets aside a couple of hours to work herself into a heightened emotional state over this, and then she triggers a release of that emotion by invoking tears or laughter. As she does so, she puts her conscious mind on "observer" mode and watches the torrent of images, words, phrases, that well up from within her, speaking aloud all that she sees and hears, and recording it on a tape player.

A while later, she returns and listens to the tape, taking not of the symbols and interpreting what they might be advising her. What does she really feel in the innermost core of her being? This fresh insight into her dilemma having been gained, she then explores the symbolic images and words for other meanings and insights relating to her deep mind and her future course of action in more general terms.

As with the more explicitly 'magical' uses of ogham introduced in the next chapter, prophecy is a technique which will yield progressively more startling results as you gain an increasing affinity with the ogham. Once the fews have become ingrained in your very being through familiarity, you will find within you a ready made "language" which your deeper mind will happily make use of to communicate its wisdom to you. You will find that the symbols which arise in prophetic utterance will readily conform to oghamic analysis, and thus you will gain considerably more from it.

The method of prophecy described here is both cathartic and can also unearth perspectives and purposes which are often concealed and "squeezed out" by everyday concerns. We all do this unconsciously at times as part of our mental housekeeping, but the technique is one that can pay dividends if practised with discipline and preparedness.

174

The Book of Ogham

Chapter 6
Magical Uses of Ogham

The ogham is more than just a system of divination, used to codify and interpret the patterns coming into manifestation in the subject's life. Once the fews have become an integral part of the way in which you view the world, they can be used in a much more dynamic fashion to actively shape and control those influences and patterns, causing happenings in the world to synchronise with your vision. Many of the old Celtic tales deal with deeds of magic, so this should come as no surprise to us. Indeed, it can be seen that the first recorded use of ogham, according to the Book of Ballymote, was a magical one, a charm devised to prevent Lugh's wife from being carried away to the Otherworld:

> B (birch) was written (seven times) to convey a warning to Lugh son of Ethliu. It was written about his wife, to prevent her from being abducted into the Otherworld (O.Ir. síd). This was seven Bs on one stave (O.Ir. flesc) of birch. (This means): Your wife will be carried away from you seven times into the Underworld or to some other land, unless she is guarded by birch.

It is recommended that newcomers to ogham should practise divination first until they achieve a measure of success with it (i.e. until the fews become a part of their own psychic make-up and really begin to "speak" to them). Successful divinatory practice also instills a very healthy respect for this flow of energy into the user before moving on to try to shape that energy in a more active fashion. Once you have experience of reading the influences represented by the ogham fews, you will be more likely to exercise due care and forethought when shaping and directing those influences to change a situation.

For simplicity of understanding, the terms "magic" and "divination" are used as if they were different things. In actuality, they are different aspects of the same thing, namely communication between the soul of the oghamist and the cosmos. As discussed in preceding chapters, a good user of ogham is in possession of a coherent mental map of his own soul and of the cosmos. In order to practise divination or magic, he enters into a state of consciousness where these two models are superimposed and he reads and directs the exchange between them. The "language" in which this exchange occurs is that of the ogham fews. In divination, he passively reads, considers and interprets the exchange and thus gains insight into what is arising in the world and how it will affect his plans. When practising magic, he actively "seeds" his mental map in the correct places / fields with those fews necessary to bear influence upon his purpose. Because his inner map is an accurate one, founded upon centuries of traditional lore and experience, affirmed by the souls of his own ancestors, the changes he makes to it strike a resonance with the outside world, and they will thus resolve themselves in our reality. The difference between divination and magic, therefore, lies simply in whether the user seeks to obtain knowledge and insight concerning a situation, or whether he seeks to alter it. The inner process is very similar. It will hopefully be obvious that before trying to change any situation, you should first understand it perfectly, otherwise you will be altering unknown variables and may bring about unforeseen and undesired results. Magic brings great responsibility and no gods or goddesses are ever going to bail you out of your own mistakes if you proceed rashly and without full knowledge.

Those readers who elect to follow the curriculum of work suggested in the next chapter will be introduced to magical techniques

The Book of Ogham

at a reasonable pace, one step at a time, and adherence to such a steady curriculum is recommended.

This chapter will suggest some ways in which the ogham fews could be employed in magical practice, all of which are methods well suited with traditional Celtic lore. The reader will have no trouble reconciling these suggested methods with the old tales, and is encouraged to search out other methods from those sources.

1. Ogham Inscription

As discussed in the first chapter, most of the surviving ogham inscriptions consist of memorials to the dead and/or celebration of ancestry. There remain a handful of examples, however, which cannot be conventionally interpreted, and which probably represent magical formulae. One of those mentioned in this context in chapter 1 is the amber bead inscribed with the fews for ATUCMLU, which was said to have healing powers and be helpful in childbirth. Let's analyse this formula and see if we can determine why it is professed to bestow these powers.

To begin our analysis, I will list the key words associated with these fews as defined in this book. This gives us a formula which incorporates the following meanings:

OBJECTIVITY - BALANCE - GATEWAY/PASSION - CREATIVITY - INWARDNESS - INSIGHT/QUICKENING - GATEWAY/PASSION

In analysing such a formula, treat it much as if it were an ogham reading. This may reveal the hidden purpose and meaning of such magical formulae. In the present case we have a head start in that we already know the type of healing powers attributed to the bead, so we can focus upon how these are expressed in the formula.

The emphasis is upon opening a gateway into the being of the possessor of the bead (U features twice in the formula), and this gateway is a vitalistic, passionate one. This also refers to birth as the gateway into life, the child being conceived in passion. In other words, it both promotes a successful birth and also reaches into its possessor's centre, stimulating their vitality and inner well-being. There is the recognition of both the objective (A) and psychosomatic (M) causes of ill-health, and the manner in which they intertwine. Both are addressed by the formula, promoting healing on all levels, inner and outer. A also refers specifically to the birth process. Balance (T) is invoked, in recognition that illness / hurt is a condition of "dis-ease", requiring adjustment back to a balanced state. The well known healing and protective powers of luise (L) are invoked, signifying a quickening process, a revivification. Finally, in the centre we find the creative impulse (C), which coupled with the life-giving and passionate emphasis explains the particular appropriateness of this formula to easing childbirth.

The above is an excellent example of an operative magical formula expressed in ogham. It should be apparent that with ingenuity and intent, a skilled user may create formulae of his/her own making for his/her own purposes. The process of inscribing such magical formulae onto appropriate materials is our first suggested method for practising oghamic magic.

The choice of material on which to carve the fews is worth consideration in every case, as different media will be suitable for different purposes. If you want to establish a permanent affirmation of some principle that is important to you, you might elect to carve it upon a stone and set it up in some high place, where it might look down upon the world, exerting its influence for years to come. If you wish to create a special amulet, such as the bead mentioned above, for purposes of healing, drawing wealth, or attracting love, then you might inscribe it upon a bracelet or some precious portable object, which you (or the person to whom you give it) can wear or carry about with you, its magic reaching out to attract the desired quality to the bearer. If you wish to influence someone (not generally recommended, since all Celtic thought champions the sovereign will of the individual and to attempt to usurp another's is to dethrone your own), you might carve the fews upon wood and bury the stave close to their home, or in a place by which they often pass. or permanent "bindings" of whatever

The Book of Ogham

nature, you might simply write the fews upon thick paper in red ink, and then burn the paper, sending the fews into the Otherworld, from where they will exert their influence. You should be creative and use a medium for each magical inscription which strikes you as being appropriate to its purpose.

The following is a suggested ritual framework which the reader can use or adapt whenever it is desired to inscribe ogham for a magical purpose. The ritual is designed to set aside a sacred place in which to work and to prepare the mind for the process of inscription, so that the essence of the ogham fews is effectively imbued into the material. The closing of the ritual then distances the oghamist from his/her work, so that the finished inscription can set about its effect unhindered.

2. Ritual Framework for Ogham Inscription

Having decided which material you wish to carve the fews upon, and having determined the ogham formula to use (a further example is suggested below), gather your utensils together at your place of working. You will require the object on which the fews are to be inscribed, a suitable tool for the inscription, and red ink to colour the fews (if appropriate to the inscribed item).

As an example, let's assume that you wish to create an amulet for personal protection against violence or accident. You decide to use a plain leather strap which can be worn around your wrist for this purpose, and choose a sharply pointed awl as a good tool to cut the fews upon it. Casting your mind over the ogham attributions, you decide that the following fews should be included in the formula:

L	luise	for its powerful protective qualities
D	duir	for its great strength and endurance
T	tinne	for its qualities of retribution upon wrongdoers
GG	gétal	for its harmonious influence
E	edad	for its property of overcoming negative situations

179

The Book of Ogham

From the above, a formula of ELDTEGGL [eldtengl] can be derived. This is pronounceable, so that it can be chanted during the inscribing process and the "key" protective few - luise - is repeated within it for emphasis.

Note: carrying a charm such as this does not obviate the necessity of taking all reasonable precautions for personal safety; it simply ensures that such precautions prove unusually successful. A "devil may care" attitude, deliberately putting yourself in danger in order to "test" the magic is a direct denial of the current of will which went into its creation, and thus counters that will and also – dangerously - insults the powers invoked in the ritual.

An open flame (a candle will be sufficient) should be on your right and an open container of water on your left. Sit or stand facing north. Then invoke the directional forces:

> Before me stands Ériu in Fal,
> on my right stands Nuada in Gor,
> on my left stands the Dagda in Mur,
> and at my back stands Lugh in Fin.
> May each bless me and go before me in all that I do
> here.

As you recite this, visualise the four towering forms surrounding you at the cardinal points of the cosmos, focusing their power toward you. The one in the north will be standing upon a stone, the one to the right will be holding a spear, the one to the left will be standing behind a cauldron, and the one behind you will be holding a sword.

Then call upon the ancestral gods and goddesses of the Celts to assist you in your work and to lay their blessing and power upon it:

> I call upon all the Gods and Goddesses on which my
> forebears called and swore their oaths. Come, be with
> me in all I do here. I call upon the Dagda, the Good
> God; upon Lugh, the Shining One; upon the strong
> Ogma; and upon Manannán of the Deep.

180

The Book of Ogham

Then speak the following invocation before actually commencing the carving of the fews:

> I call upon you, the three Brigids, to guide my hands and the ogham fews. I call upon you, the three Morríghna, to guide my hand that I may make the fews good and true.

Then take up the substance to be carved and the inscribing tool and cut the stemline along which the fews will be carved, adding the feather mark at the starting point of the inscription. Carefully inscribe each few in its turn, whispering or "singing" its name as you cut it. Let your hot breath pass over the fews, imbuing them with life force. Once the ogham formula has been inscribed, colour it with red ink (if appropriate; a stone or stave of wood could be so coloured; a piece of jewellery or other decorative item probably should not). Hold the finished object in your hands (or place your hands upon it if it is too large / heavy to hold), just under your mouth and chant the formula under your breath, over and over. After a time, your mind will enter a trancelike state, and the chanting will become automatic. At this point, your work is done and you should "snap out of it".

In order to finally "ground" the magic of the formula in the item, mentally recite the formula as you sprinkle th object with water from the bowl, and pass it through the flame. This removes all influences from it except for the magical force of the inscribed formula.

Having prepared the item in this way, gather up your things, express your thanks to the gods and goddesses you called upon for assistance, and loudly clap your hands or stamp your feet to reestablish yourself back in the world of mundane things. The prepared item can now be worn, given or placed as appropriate to its use, and left to get on with its business. You should leave it be and not dwell upon it further until your desired results manifest themselves.

Note: Beginners at magical practice would do well to stick with the above framework for their early experiments. Indeed, even advanced practitioners should discipline themselves to follow such a set procedure in most instances. As your skill grows, however, you are bound to find yourself in those situations when you need to accomplish some shift in the prevailing circumstances right here and now and cannot really wait until you get home to your accustomed place of working. As experience grows, you will find that you are able to slip into an altered state of consciousness and direct the ogham streams from within with ever increasing perception and intensity. You may find that when real need arises it may be sufficient to simply quickly write a formula in ogham on a piece of paper with no preamble at all in order to achieve needed rapid results. Indeed, a truly experienced oghamist should be able to simply whisper a formula under his/her breath, visualising the fews as fiery strokes in the air before him/her in order to get results, without need for any tangible inscription.

If you find any affinity with ogham, you can reasonably expect to ultimately develop such "quick fire" abilities. It cannot be stressed enough, however, that the powerful focus of mind and inner resonance required for such work arises only out of prior painstaking practice, and that even when attained it is a good idea to keep up the full process of the ritual whenever possible, otherwise the magical "muscles" become lazy.

3. Bardic Poetry

Among the Celts, the process of storytelling was not simply a means of entertainment, nor was it merely a means to keep cultural identity alive. The telling of a story was perceived as an active magical operation, which bestowed a tangible blessing upon the teller of the tale and upon those who listened to it. (See Celtic Heritage by Alwyn and Brinley Rees for a fuller development of this theme.)

In similar fashion, the tales tell that when a bard recited before the king, the tale or poem served to exalt the king in the sight of his people, to extend his rule and influence. Tales are also told, however, which reveal how a corrupt ruler could be subjected to

182

The Book of Ogham

satirical poetry by the bard, which would have the effect of raising physical boils upon the king's skin, ridiculing and lessening him in the eyes of his subjects (it was very important to the Celts that their king should be without blemish).

From this pattern we can reconstruct a further magical application of the ogham fews, but one which directly employs their sonic qualities. The carved shapes, after all, are only ways of codifying and arranging the sounds which they represent. Among a musical and poetic people such as the Celts, the sound rather than the image is the primary symbol. In order to use this magical technique, it is necessary to recite a poem which encapsulates our intention and also stresses the sounds of the few(s) appropriate to the magical purpose. We are not interested here in rhyming poetry, but in alliterative poetry, i.e. poetry which gains its emphasis from the repeated use of certain letters at the beginning of words. For example, the word "begin" alliterates with "birch" and "birth".

The poem can be devised within a formal ritual setting by following steps identical to those described for the inscriptions above, simply substituting the creation of the poem for the process of inscribing fews on a material object.

What happens next depends upon your desired purpose and the circumstances surrounding the situation you wish to influence. If you wish to influence a place or region, the best thing to do is create your poem, then go to the place or region and actually recite the poem there. Similarly, if you seek to influence a person, for best effect and "linking" you should recite the poem in his or her presence. This would ideally be done audibly, but could be muttered under your breath if needs must. If this direct link recital cannot be achieved for some reason (and laziness is not a reason you should allow yourself to accept), then the poem must be recited with will and feeling in the context of the ritual at which it is created. If a place is the focus, you should have an appropriate photograph or map to hand to concentrate your mind upon. If a person is the focus, you must have a photograph of them to hand, or some object (such as a signature) intimately linked with them.

Note that it is not necessary to attain to Shakespearean

standards in your composition, as long as you are confident you have done the best you can. Here follows a simple example poem to attract the force of change into a person's life if a feeling of stasis or of going nowhere fast comes over you. As such, it is based around the R-few:

> Right wretched the road that roves round and round,
> Rarely reaching new regions.
> I ride a new route, I roam a new range,
> I arrive in rolling new realms.

With practice and familiarity with the technique, you will want to produce more complex poems, incorporating the combined influence of several fews, weaving in and out of the poem's spoken spell. Indeed, a time will come when the actual words of the poem matter little and it will be possible to recite a poem seemingly in praise of something whilst the actual oghams alliterated within the verse are directed at thwarting and entangling the situation.

This magical method relies heavily upon your own creativity, and can be extremely rewarding in a whole spectrum of ways. The beginner need not be cowed by the challenge, ability will arise spontaneously and enthusiastically with continued application. The curriculum in the next chapter will assist in developing the skills for this sort of magical work in a measured, step by step fashion.

4. Journeying to the Otherworld

One of the distinguishing features of Celtic mythical tales is the immanence of other worlds, other realities, which the adventurer can slip into unawares and there experience strange and life-changing events. This technique of tale weaving has in more recent years been superbly recreated by the author Robert Holdstock in his book Mythago Wood and subsequent novels.

Otherworld journeys can be woven into oghamic magical work with a little thought and preparation. They are very easy to set up, but require some considerable practice to get right. There are two distinct ways of undertaking such journeys, one of which is familiar, whilst the other is fairly unique to Celtic practice.

The first, more familiar, technique is similar to other methods of astral or shamanic journeys, or pathworkings. In such cases, the practitioner uses his/her visual imagination to create an inner landscape, which he/she explores to gain insight. For instance, an ogham few could be used as an imaginary doorway, which you would "step through" in your mind's eye in order to explore what lay behind. Here you would find a land which would be flavoured by the meaning and correspondences of that ogham and here you could discover new secrets about the few, presented to you by your deep mind in this symbolic inner landscape. You might also meet entities, deities or heroes attributed to the few with whom you could converse.

The other kind of Otherworld journey is not a purely inward experience, but is tied in with a journey in the outer, objective world.

In its simplest form, plan a journey in your locality. It may be a trip to the top of a mountain, a walk along a woodland path, or a visit to a nearby sacred site. Plan the trip in your mind, and prepare yourself to be receptive to Otherworldly influences. Decide at which point in the journey you will step into the Otherworld.

Then begin your journey (start practising with relatively short ones, perhaps and hour's walk). With every step along the path, heighten your sensitivity and allow your mind to open. During the actual journey, you must not question what happens, merely accept and remember it. Critical analysis is important, but the time for that is afterwards, not during.

At the predetermined point, allow your senses to blur as you step beyond ordinary physical reality. The remainder of the journey is walked in an altered state of consciousness in which everything seen and experienced is interpreted as a directly meaningful communication to your own soul. When familiar with the practice, you may seem to encounter non-human entities who may offer assistance or provide information. These manifestations should be accepted at face value at the time, and only critically examined afterwards. They are most likely manifestations of the deep places of

The Book of Ogham

your own mind, but even if this is so they can only communicate with you if you accept them as objectively real at the time. Turn critical thought upon them during the experience and their potency and value will dissipate as their source is blocked by cruder thought patterns. I would also caution the cocky adventurer who thinks he/she has an answer for everything – beware, not all manifestations will fit into this category. There are indeed more things walking the worlds than you have dreamed of.

When you reach the destination of your journey, state your intent clearly, honour your ancestral gods, and ensure that you leave a gift in exchange for the gifts you have received. Then retrace your steps, allowing normal consciousness to gradually return, until you reach the predetermined gateway point once more and step back into the world of men.

A great many magical applications of this technique will become apparent to you, and in particular it is a wonderful way to explore and integrate the ogham fews. You can take a journey in suitable surroundings with the express purpose of investigating the hidden secrets of each ogham in turn. You may also wish to use the diagram of the worlds printed on pages 51 and 52 to tread the ogham paths to the cities and mounds of the sidhe. But it is important to begin easily, to practise the technique with gentler journeys first until a degree of success and a high degree of synchronicity is regularly attainable.

It should be noted that although I have referred to the Otherworld as a catch-all term throughout these paragraphs, the technique applies equally to the Underworld. It is easy to make too glib and simplistic a differentiation between the two, but for our present purposes I will cautiously and inadequately suggest that the Otherworld is best used to gain insight and knowledge and assistance, whereas the Underworld is a place to face initiatory trials and to plant mysterious seeds which may bear mysterious fruit in time to come. Experiment and learn.

The Book of Ogham

5. The Geis and its Magical Application

A spirit of antinomianism – the breaking of cultural taboos – is an essential element in bringing about the transformations sought by the modern day druid. There is, however, also another type of taboo which is quite specific to Celtic practice, one which relates solely to and individual rather than to a culture or society; this the Celts termed a geis (pl. geisa).

A geis was the price a hero paid for his heroism, the price for his prowess and immortalisation in tales. The principle at work here is similar to that expressed in the Germanic account of Odin, who won the runes by a sacrifice of himself to Himself. By deliberately offering up the lesser thing, the hero gains the greater thing in exchange.

A geis can take many forms. It is an emphatic denial of certain activities, or – less often – an insistence upon certain activities. These prohibitions did not always make apparent sense. After all, there is little magical virtue or vigilance in doing something which is pure common sense, or somehow praiseworthy, anyway. A geis is something out of the ordinary, something which requires constant vigilance so as not to be caught transgressing it unawares. For example, some of the geisa of Conaire included such demands that he must not be away from Tara for nine nights in succession; that he must not settle the quarrel of any two of his serfs; that he must not spend the night in a house from which firelight can be seen after sunset and into which one can see from outside.

In return for these strange observances, the hero possessed superhuman qualities. The greater the geisa, the greater the power. The geisa were also used as omens of doom by the storytellers, and listeners could sense the hero's death approaching as one by one each geis was violated. Occasionally a hero would be caught in a trap, checkmated between two of his geisa, as when CúChulainn passes a fire where a dog is being roasted: he has a geis that he must never eat dog, and another that he must never pass a cooking hearth without eating the food which is being coked thereon. These moments of Fate / Destiny are special applications of the "in-between", "no-time",

187

The Book of Ogham

"no-place" mysteries of the Celtic tradition, which are discussed further below.

A geis fulfills three valuable magical functions:

1. It instills a sense of honour, of principle. It tests the mettle of the individual by demanding honourable action and adherence to principle even when it is inconvenient. The geis strengthens the will by creating a magical obligation that the recipient will have the courage and determination to adhere to a willed code of conduct instead of crumbling at the slightest test.
2. It promotes vigilance and wakefulness. Especially when a geis is complex or disarmingly unusual, it requires a high degree of mental alertness to remain constantly on guard against transgressing it.
3. It is a sacrifice of the lesser to the greater. By willfully setting aside certain distractions in life, it is possible to focus attention much more clearly upon meaningful visions and goals. The energy and time liberated provide a tremendous boost to progress.

The reader will doubtless think of other benefits, which will probably be worthwhile elaborations or combination of the above.

The foregoing is all very well, but how to have a geis bestowed on you? If you are in a teacher / student relationship, you may ask your mentor to decide upon a suitable geis for you. Alternatively, you may ask a close friend to select some suitable abstention or commitment for you (it should suit the spirit of traditional geisa and not be something of obvious moral or practical value; it is intended to be an observation of a magical discipline, and any secondary benefits would detract from this).If you have nobody that you can rely upon to place a suitable geis upon you, you can carry out a ritual according to the style suggested earlier in this chapter. Instead of charging ogham fews at the focal point, however, call out to your ancestral gods to bestow a geis upon you. The ritual done, go out and interpret the first thing that happens to you as an indicator of your geis. If you find yourself holding a door open for someone, for instance, you might interpret your geis as being that you must always ensure that you are the last person in the group you are with to enter a room.

Although not directly linked to the ogham, the acceptance of geisa by advanced practitioners will greatly strengthen their overall link with the Celtic tradition, and will increase their magical and divinatory prowess in general. Do be aware that a geis should not be sought lightly, and once obtained it can never be cast off without inviting very hard consequences. It is strongly advised that much soul searching should be carried out before taking on a geis. If you follow the curriculum described in the next chapter, you will notice that the adoption of geisa is not advised until the very last stage.

A Note on Magical Times and Places

The timing of magical workings can greatly aid their effectiveness if the practitioner deliberately selects a time and a place which are meaningful and with which he/she feels a resonance, an affinity, supplying a subjective boost to any ritual performed there. One of the key components in Celtic myth – and thus in Celtic magical practice – is the emphasis upon those times and places which are somehow "in-between", which are not this and not that, neither one thing nor the other.

These "in betweens" are often times of transition, such as dawn and dusk, or the boundaries between the land, the sea and the sky. These are times and places which are in a state of change, moving from one condition to another. As such, they are yet unshaped and highly malleable. Those times of the year marked by the Celtic festivals provide excellent working dates, as do traditional sacred sites such as groves and stone circles. Once the simple principles of flux and balance are understood, however, you may find yourself able to take advantage of more localised phenomena in like fashion.

To perform magic at these in between times at in between places is to reinforce the separation of the magician from the mechanics of the cosmos, and to invoke a matrix in which the forces of change may more readily affect the universe while it is in a state of flux.

The example of the death of Lleu Llaw Gyffes illustrates this point, as he could not be slain either inside or outside a house, neither on horseback, nor on foot, neither in water nor on land, neither clothed nor unclothed. He is ultimately wounded severely when in between these several opposites, when he is half dressed after taking a bath in a tub beneath a thatched frame on a river bank, standing with one foot on the back of a goat and the other on the edge of the tub. Death through multiple causes, seemingly mutually exclusive, is a common feature in Celtic symbolism. When we step into those areas where boundaries merge, seemingly impossible things can happen.

Not only Fate manifests itself through these twilight times and places, of course. The power of will may also do so. I encourage readers to experiment with these ideas in their magical experiments. Such efforts will prove remarkably worthwhile.

The Book of Ogham

Chapter 7
An Oghamic Study Curriculum

The beginner may be wondering how best to start working with the ogham. There is a lot of material in this book; how should one start to assimilate it? At what stage should study lead into more directly practical work? At what stage should the student feel confident to try using the ogham fews for specifically magical purposes?

The best approach to the study and use of ogham is tackled on a regular, daily basis: diary work. Although this approach can sometimes seem tedious, it does get results, and it gets them quickly, consistently and effectively. I therefore suggest the following curriculum of regular work as a simple and measured way of learning and applying the heart of the ogham system.

It should be understood from the outset that this is a living system, which will develop slightly differently for each individual as it is worked with. Experienced students may introduce subtle alterations once they have absorbed the essence of the system.

Regular application in a curriculum such as this is essential. However, everyone is inevitably going to miss a day from time to time as circumstances dictate. When this happens, do not recriminate yourself, just resume working again as soon as you are able. This is not a licence to laziness, but you should acknowledge your weaknesses

191

The Book of Ogham

as well as your strengths. If you fall, pick yourself up and carry on cheerfully.

The curriculum is in a series of carefully measured steps. You should tackle them each in turn and deal with each new aspect of the work in its due place. You will then become proficient with the oghams and they will flow as living streams from the core of your being out into the world and back again. By the time you reach more advanced work, it will be second nature to you already.

STAGE 1

1. You should endeavour to read as much as you can on the subject of Celtic myth and magic (the bibliography at the close of this book will be helpful in selecting suitable texts).

2. You should spend nine days in intense meditation upon the meaning of each ogham character in turn. At this stage of the work, this should include absorption and internalisation of the meanings given for each of the fews in this book. You should also write down any personal insights arising from your thoughts upon those meanings, plus any insights gained from other sources. The amount of time spent in such intense thought each day will vary from student to student, but a good guideline will be not less than ten minutes per day, resulting in ninety minutes' intensive meditation upon each character during this first step of the work. Affording nine days' study to each ogham few will result in a total span of $20 \times 9 = 180$ days for the main ogham characters, plus another $5 \times 9 = 45$ days for the forfedha, for a total of 225 days for Step 1 of the curriculum.

3. At least once every week during this step of the work, the student should carry out a divinatory reading using the ogham, employing the divinatory methods and meanings suggested in this book.

4. At some stage during this phase, the student should select and 'charge' a suitable site for outdoor working, a personal place of power.

   Celtic magic has always been associated with the notion

192

The Book of Ogham

of "sacred sites", most notably the great stone circles and alignments, such as the famous Stonehenge on England's Salisbury Plain. The Celtic countries are actually host to many hundreds of these ancient monuments, any of which can provide a valuable magical link. The Celts did not build most of these monuments, but these pre-Celtic structures were seen as gates to the Underworld and/or Otherworld in the Celtic mind.

Not everyone is lucky enough to live within easy reach of good examples of such places, however. Such will have to try a little bit harder to identify suitable places for those magical workings why cry out for a sacred place to use as a focus of power. Even those who have a stone circle or sacred grove on their doorsteps, however, will find it next to useless without understanding those keys which render such places potent.

Selection of a location basically depends upon the recognition that there are certain places whose locality and geometry simply have an "atmosphere" which stimulates the psyche. Such an area might lie in a hollow, or it may be an elevated spot; in either case, the interplay between sky and earth will be enhanced in the mind's eye. There may be bizarre angular features in the terrain, or an unnaturally shaped surface. Gnarled and twisted trees suggest primeval landscapes, then of course there are the old crossroads and haunted spots favoured by the later grimoire traditions.

Whatever stimulates your mind and turns it to magic, that's what you need to look for. This is a very subjective thing as regards preference for eerie, haunting forests or stark, monolithic simplicity. Try looking for weird angles, serpentine curves, zigzags; anything evocative that draws the eye repeatedly to it. Be aware of shapes and contours, not just surface textures and general scenery details.

Once you have found a suitable location for your work, you now need to define the space and set it aside as sacred, a place of the mysteries. Traditional stone circles, etc., already have this hard work done, of course, but you still have to make the markers your own. If there are no such markers already present, your job

193

of of making the place your own may actually be easier rather than harder, as you can select your own markers and not have to rationalise someone else's. These markers need not necessarily be erected within the working area itself. You may choose instead to use landmarks on the horizon which are either significant in some way in their own right, or whose geometric configuration is pleasing and appropriate. In your mind's eye, these distant features can be used to define a much smaller, localised space, that one spot at which you intuitively feel their influences converge.

Now follows the most important part of creating a space set aside for magical work: establishing a resonance between the atmosphere / ambiance of the place and your own psyche. Properly established and subjectively empowered, such a site will be an inspirational force in your work. Without this synchronisation, it is just another patch of dirt.

How to do this? Any way that suggests itself to your own creative genius will be appropriate, but personally I like the vigil. This involves spending a period of time – typically overnight – alone in the designated place. This vigil will be fruitful or not, depending upon the will, determination and imagination you bring to it. Sit or stand there alone in the darkness, soaking in the atmosphere and internalising it, waiting for the sign that your work is done, that illuminating flash connecting your own soul with the site. This will come as an almost physical sensation of certainty and understanding. I usually experience such moments as a sudden pressure in the pit of my stomach, coupled with a deep inner conviction. Your response may be different. It is nice then to wait and watch the sun rise, directing its first rays upon you and the site, then make your way home to catch up on your sleep.

Your special place will be a support for your work for many years to come, somewhere to go when you need direct illumination.

STAGE 2

The Book of Ogham

By now, the basic meanings and order of the ogham fews should be lodged within your mind's structure. The true numinous apprehension of each few may not yet have been achieved, but with solid work the student is laying the ground for it, and truly personal insights may now be beginning to appear in relation to the oghams. This second stage builds upon the work done in the first stage and deepens the mental apprehension of the fews, adding scope for a more personal touch.

1. During this stage, ten days should be spent in renewed intensive meditation upon each of the 20 main ogham fews (excluding the forfedha). That is 200 days for this stage in total.
2. Begin each day with a few minutes' reflection upon the notes you made during the first stage about the meaning of the few you will be meditating upon that day.
3. Obtain a dictionary for one of the Q-Celtic languages (Irish, Scottish or Manx Gaelic). Search through the dictionary to find a Gaelic word which begins with, or somehow stresses, the sound represented by that day's ogham few. Take your time and find a word whose meaning really seems to have an affinity with the few in your eyes. Choose a different word every day over the ten day period allotted to that few, learn them by heart, and carefully consider the bearing of each word upon the meaning of the few. Strive to perceive the "larger picture" presented by the combined meanings of these selected words.

    For example, consider the following sampling of Manx words beginning with the B sound:

    > Bea = Life
    > Barriaght = Victory
    > Bann = to Bless
    > Bioid = Liveliness
    > Blaaghey = Blossoming, flowering, budding, flourishing

4. Close the day's work with the following words:

The Book of Ogham

"I dedicate this work to my own immortal self, that I may understand all that I have been and all that I yet may be. I call upon the gods and goddesses of my ancestors to witness my dedication and commitment. May the doors to the mounds of the Sidhe be opened to me."

5. Continue with a minimum of one ogham divination every week. Be sure to gain familiarity with all of the different methods of reading.

6. At an appropriate time during this second stage of the work, carry out the following special rite of awakening.

The ritual should be carried out on three successive nights. On each occasion you should go to the sacred place prepared in stage 1 and call upon your ancestral gods, as outlined in the chapter on magical practice. Having done so, on the first night you should relive some mythical event which speaks to you of the essence of Celtic magic which you seek to recapture. The play must be complete, you should recreate and reenact every role in the drama, reliving every emotion, every thought, until the mystery of your chosen myth is understood. On the second night, consider your goals and motivations in studying the ogham. Invoke the mythic quality you identified the previous night and bind it to your considered purposes and personal goals. Swear an oath that you will embody this quality and reawaken the ways and works of your ancestors in the world. On the third night, be still and quiet in your sacred place and carefully open your mind to that which you have awakened. Let your ancestors and the Sidhe come to you and touch your consciousness, imparting their wisdom. You have awakened yourself, and in doing so, you have awakened them. Their assistance will strengthen and empower you.

STAGE 3

At this stage, the intention is to deepen the student's empathy with the

196

The Book of Ogham

ogham on a practical level. We will therefore be pushing further into magical practice, and beginning preliminary practice with the fundamentals of bardic poetry.

1. In order to truly familiarise yourself with the sound qualities of the oghams and their interplay, and the ways in which these things were experienced in the Celtic psyche, you should really begin serious study of one of the Gaelic languages. It is up to you whether you opt to attend classes or use one of the many excellent home study packs, as long as you have the discipline to stick with it.

2. You should practise "singing" the sounds of the fews, spending ten days on each, for a total of 200 days. You may emphasise either the primary sound of the few or its actual name, or indeed a combination. Here follows an example of how you might intone the B-few:

> "Beh beh beh beh beh
> beithe beithe beithe
> beh beh beh
> beithe"

You should spend a minimum of ten minutes per day in such singing practice, and you should carry out at least one of your daily exercises in your sacred place at least once each fortnight.

3. You should now decide upon some areas of your life where you need to make changes, and you should follow the instructions in the chapter on magical practice to assist you in inscribing oghams in order to create definite changes in your life. The exact purposes and motivations will obviously be up to yourself. Where possible, such magical operations should be carried out at your sacred place (though this will not always be practical; use your best judgement).

4. You should practise writing alliterative poetry, whose secret keys and inner meanings are revealed by the accentuated letters. At this practice stage, you should write a poem to describe the

197

influence of each ogham few in turn. Spend ten days on each few
to develop each poem fully. It is helpful to spend the first day of
each ten day period collecting a lot of usable words, with the
correct sound value and meaning, from a dictionary. The best of
these words can then be woven into an alliterative poem.

Here follows an example for sail:

> "Sable shadows, silence-shrouded
> Sit beneath the sally-tree.
> Shifting shapes that ghostly shimmer
> And slowly stir the still, deep places,
> Shades beneath the surface of the mind."

STAGE 4

1. Spend ten days on each few, meditating specifically upon the
   symbolism of the word oghams of Morainn mac Moin, Maic ind
   Oc and CúChulainn, as listed under the ogham descriptions in
   chapter 4. These rediscovered keys of the earliest perceptions of
   the fews will assist you in winning to their true meanings. You
   should consider the symbolism of each word ogham in turn and
   relate it to what you already know of the few: how does it shed
   new light upon your insights? What new qualities does it suggest?
   Then try to integrate all three sets of word oghams in a single
   vision in order to get a new, numinous perception of the fews. Be
   aware that you are working with the same coded meanings that
   your ancestors used; the sense of continuity will be of considerable
   assistance. This should keep you busy for 200 days.
2. If you have not already done so, now is definitely the time to
   fabricate a personalised set of ogham fews, hand carved from a
   suitable wood as described in chapter 5.
3. Read as many authentic Celtic tales as you can which deal with the
   Otherworld and/or Underworld in their various aspects. This will
   be good preparation for the journeying exercises in step 5.
4. Now that you have experience in the magical use of ogham

198

inscriptions, and have tried your hand at writing alliterative poetry, it is time to begin using bardic poetry in order to achieve your magical goals and initiate your planned life changes. Do your preparations at home, but try to write the finished version of at least some of your compositions at your sacred place, as this will increase both their own effectiveness and the power of the site in your own mind. Also, don't forget that for our ancestors, the recital of a poem was more important than the process of writing it down. Verbal and sonic magic was a far more frequent and puissant occurrence than carved or written inscriptions, so declare your poems to the world.

STAGE 5

Continue your revision of all you have previously learned, and continue practicing your divinatory readings and magical practices.
You should use the guidelines for Otherworld journeys given in the previous chapter to deliberately plan journeys with the express purpose of exploring the inner meanings of each ogham few in turn. By referring to the cosmological diagrams in chapter 2, you can see which realms each few connects to, which should give you clues to the type of journey to expect in each case, as should the correspondences listed for each few in chapter 4. You may choose to employ either form of journey, whether you travel on the imaginative plane, journeying in your mind's inner eye, or superimpose an Otherworldly interpretation upon a physical walk. Really, you should seek proficiency with both methods. In either case, you should by now be fairly well skilled in interpreting ogham symbolism , and you will find that your consciousness respects that and offers insights in forms you will be likely to understand.
Now is the time to pursue true heroism if you so desire: seek out a geis as suggested in the previous chapter.
Finally, to close the curriculum, you should devise a task for yourself connected to the ogham in particular or to the Celtic tradition in general. This task will constitute a kind of "master work" to mark

The Book of Ogham

your mastery over the oghams. t will be unique in all cases, and there is no point in anticipating what it may be until you get there. The choice and execution of a master work is reliant upon having completed the curriculum first. It should be some deed, craft, or new (or rediscovered) learning, which will stand as a permanent testimony to your genius. You will then be worthy of the title of druid.

The Book of Ogham

Appendix One
Oghamic Table of Correspondences

I	II	III	IV	V
No.	Shape	Sound Value	Original Ogham Name	Meaning of Name
1		B	beithe	birch-tree
2		L	luise, or lus	flame, radiance or plant, herb, vegetable
3		F	fern	alder-tree
4		S	sail	willow-tree
5		N	nin	forked branch, lofty
6		H	úath	fear, horror
7		D	duir	oak-tree
8		T	tinne	bar, rod of metal, ingot, mass of molten metal
9		C	coll	hazel
10		Q	cert	bush, rag
11		M	muin	neck, trick, love
12		G	gort	field
13		GG	gétal	(act of) wounding, slaying
14		Z	sraib, or straif	sulphur
15		R	ruise	reddening
16		A	ailm	pine-tree (?)
17		O	onn	ash-tree
18		U	úr, úir	earth, soil, grave
19		E	éo > edad	salmon
20		I	éo > idad	yew-tree

201

The Book of Ogham

	VI	VII	VIII
	Word Ogham of Morainn mac Moin	Word Ogham of Maic ind Oc	Word Ogham of CúChulainn
B	Withered foot with fine hair	Greyest of skin	Beauty of the eyebrow
L	Lustre of the eye	Friend of cattle	Sustenance of cattle
F	Vanguard of the warrior-band	Container of milk	Protection of the heart
S	Pallor of a dead man	Sustenance of bees	Beginning of honey
N	Establishing of peace	Boast of women	Boast of beauty
H	Assembly of packs of hounds	Blanching of faces	Most difficult at night
D	Most exalted tree	Handicraft of an artificer	Most carved of craftsmanship
T	One of three parts of a wheel	Marrow of coal	One of three parts of a wagon
C	Fairest tree	Friend of nutshells	Sweetest tree
Q	Shelter of a lunatic	Substance of an insignificant person	Dregs of clothing
M	Strongest in exertion	Proverb of slaughter	Path of the voice
G	Sweetest grass	Suitable place for cows	Sating of multitudes
GG	Sustenance of a leech	Raiment of physicians	Beginning of slaying
Z	Strongest reddening	Increase of secrets	Seeking of clouds
R	Most intense blushing	Reddening of faces	Glow of anger
A	Loudest groan	Beginning of an answer	Beginning of a calling
O	Wounder of horses	Smoothest of Craftsmanship	Sustaining of warrior-bands
U	In cold dwellings	Propagation of plants	Shroud of a dead man
E	Discerning tree	Exchange of friends	Brother of birch
I	Oldest tree	Fairest of the ancients	Energy of an infirm person

The Book of Ogham

	IX	X	XI		XII	XIII
	Later Tree-Name	Translated Tree-Name	Inner Meaning		Colours* (O.Ir.)	Translation of Colours
1	beith	birch	Vitality		ban	white
2	luis	rowan	Insight/Quickening		liath	grey
3	fern	alder	Foundation		flann	red
4	sail	willow	Intuition		sodath	fine-coloured
5	nin	ash	Rebirth		necht	clear
6	huath	whitethorn	Misfortune		huath	"terrible"
7	duir	oak	Endurance		dub	black
8	tinne	holly	Balance		temen	dark grey
9	coll	hazel	Creativity		cron	brown
10	queirt	apple	Beauty/Eternity		quair	mouse-coloured
11	muin	vine	Inwardness		mbracht	variegated
12	gort	ivy	Development		gorm	blue
13	ngetal	broom	Harmony		nglas	green
14	straif	blackthorn	Control		sorcha	bright
15	ruis	elder	Change		ruadh	red
16	ailm	fir	Objectivity		alad	piebald
17	onn	furze	Wisdom/Synthesis		odhar	dun
18	ur	heather	Gateway/Passion		usgdha	resinous
19	edad	aspen	Overcoming		erc	red
20	idad	yew	Death/Immortality		irfind	very white

* Note that the Book of Ballymote also contains a section called "Sow Ogham", which ascribes a colour to each of the five vertical columns so that the first character in each aicme is white, the second grey, the third black, the fourth amber and the fifth blue.

The Book of Ogham

	XIV	XV	XVI	XVII
	Birds	Translation of Birds	Arts and Crafts	Translation of Arts
1	besan	pheasant	bethumnacht	livelihood
2	lachan	duck	lumnacht	pilotage
3	faelinn	gull	filideacht	poetry
4	seg	hawk	sairsi	handicraft
5	naescu	snipe	notaireacht	notary work
6	hadaig	night raven	h-airchetal	trisyllabic poetry
7	droen	wren	druidheacht	wizardry
8	truith	starling	tornoracht	turning
9	?*	?*	cruitireacht	harping
10	querc	hen	quislenacht	fluting
11	mintan	titmouse	milaideacht	soldiering
12	geis	swan	gaibneacht	smithwork
13	ngeigh	goose	ngibae	modeling
14	stmolach	thrush	sreghuindeacht	deer stalking
15	rocnat	small rook	ronaireacht	dispensing
16	aidhircleog	lapwing	airigeacht	sovereignty
17	odoroscrach	scrat (?)	ogmoracht	harvesting
18	uiseog	lark	umaideacht	brasswork
19	ela	swan	enaireacht	fowling
20	illait	eaglet	(1) iascaireacht (2) ibroracht	(1) fishing (2) yew woodwork

* Missing in the list found in the text of the Auraicept na N'Eces.

204

The Book of Ogham

GLOSSARY

In the phonetic transcriptions of the Irish words and names which follow, the spelling dh = the "th" sound as in "then".

aicme [acme]: A family or group of five ogham fews.

Beltaine [BELT-en-a]: Major Celtic vernal fire festival. Modern "ay Eve".

bith [bith]: The world, or the manifest physical universe.

blath [blath]: Prosperity. A quality describing the eastern realm among the fifths.

Book of Ballymote: A 14th Century Irish manuscript containing the greatest collection of ogham lore of any O.Ir. text.

cath [cath]: Conflict. A quality describing the northern realm among the fifths.

Caillach [kahll-yakh or kell-ey]: Common name for the divine hag in Irish lore.

Dagda [doy-da]: The Good God. The god of the druids.

ebad [evadh]: Name of the forfidh corresponding to the sovereign centre (mide). Its sound value is [ea] and its name means aspen". This is also another name for the E-few.

few: An Anglicised form of the Irish fidh.

fianna [FEE-enna]: A wandering band of warrior-bards. Their most famous leader was Finn mac Cumhaill. They correspond to the Erulian bands in Germanic tradition.

fidh, pl. fedha [fidh; fedha]: Irish word for "wood" or "tree", used to denote the ogham characters – as well as the trees they represent.

Fifth: A "province" of the land or cosmos. Irish coiced, a fifth.

fis [fish]: Learning. A quality describing the western realm among the fifths.

fili, pl. filid [filee; fileedh]: The Irish term which answers most closely to the term "druid".

flesc [flesk]: The stemline.

forfidh, pl. forfedha [for-fidh; for-fedha]: The additional five fews which are used for diphthongs, and which are used to symbolise the five provinces.

geis, pl. geisa [gay-sh; gay-sha]: A kind of "taboo" in Celtic lore which is typically a prohibition against doing something, but which is at the same time a source of power.

iphin [ifin]: Name of the forfidh corresponding to the north (cath). Its sound value is [io] and its name means "gooseberry".

Lugh [lugh or loo]: The Celtic god of magic, war and the arts. His emblematic weapon is the spear. In many ways he answers to the Germanic god Woden.

mag (or magh) [moy]: A plane or field. Used of the higher or "Otherworlds".

mide [midh-e]: "The Middle". See also rige.

Mórríghan: "The Great Queen", or "Queen of Phantoms".

morrighna [mor-righna]: A collective name for the three-aspected form of Mórríghan, which also includes Nemain and either Badb or Macha.

nemeton: Celtic term for a sacred grove and enclosure.

notch: The short lines or dots used to indicate the vowels of the ogham system.

oir [or]: Name of the forfidh corresponding to the south (seis). Its sound value is [oi] and its name means "spindle".

Ogma: The Irish hero whose name is represented in the name of the oghams. He is the Irish Hercules. The Gaulish form of his name is Ogmios.

Otherworld: A collective name for the celestial or "higher" realm(s) in the Celtic cosmology. These are most often designated with names with the Irish word magh (plain) in them.

phagos [faghos]: Name of the forfidh corresponding to the east (blath). Originally this seems to have been a Greek word. Its sound value is [ae] and its name means "beech".

rige [ree-a]: Sovereignty. A quality describing the middle realm, or the mide of the fifths.

Samhain (also Samain) [saw-en]: "The End of Summer", the major Celtic autumnal fire festival. Modern "Hallowe'en".

score: The lines which cross the stemline to form the ogham fews.

seis [shesh]: Harmony. A quality describing the southern realm among the fifths.

sídhe (or síd) [shee]: The realm of the dead, the "fairy realm", or the Underworld in Celtic lore.

stemline: The straight line on which the notches and scores are cut to make the ogham fews.

tír [teer]: This word generally means "land", but also is used symbolically for names of the Underworld.

uileand [ulen]: Name of the forfidh corresponding to the west (fis). Its name means "honeysuckle".

Underworld: A collective name for the chthonic or "lower" realm(s) in the Celtic cosmology. These are most often designated with names with the Irish word tír (land) in them.

The Book of Ogham

The Book of Ogham

Afterword

The system presented in this book provides the bare bones of an authentically Celtic philosophy and methodology. In these pages the reader will find a series of "keys of knowledge" which will unlock the mysteries of the Celtic world to the seeking mind if applied with precision. Nevertheless, this present volume does not pretend to reveal the entirety of Celtic philosophy. That can only be won by the individual by application of a twofold process:

1. Study of the ancient tales of the Celts, and application of the keys found in this book to unlock the hidden meanings behind the symbolism of these stories. This is too vast a study for a volume such as the present one, and such work is in any case eminently more satisfying when the secrets are won for oneself.

2. Observation of the patterns represented by the oghams as they manifest in one's own life, and manipulation of these patterns of manifestation through operative use of the oghams. This experience of the living current of the oghams will shed light upon your data obtained from other sources, and vice versa.

It should by now be obvious that the purpose of studying the oghams is to awaken you to the large patterns which move through life on both a personal and a cosmic scale. The oghams represent the unfolding of these forces. By recognising them aright, you gain insight into the world which would ordinarily pass by unnoticed, and these insights afford the possibility of altering the patterns of manifestation

The Book of Ogham

in subtle ways beneficial to you.

The key to success with the ogham system, therefore, lies in internalising the oghams until you are able to see past the visual, auditory and numeric symbols to determine the true reality which lies beneath them. Once this vibrant level of understanding and direct apprehension has been attained, you will truly walk with the sidhe.

Michael Kelly
Ramsey, Isle of Man
Lugnasadh, 1999

The Book of Ogham

Pronunciation of Old Irish

Irish is a difficult language to pronounce correctly because the way the words are written often bear little resemblance to the way they would seem to be pronounced from an English perspective. However, once some practice and familiarity with the spelling system is gained, it will be found to be easier than it might have appeared at first.

Most readers will have seen certain Irish words in at least two different spelling systems. For example, one might see "Samain" in one place and "Samhain" in another. The former is the true Old Irish orthography, while the latter is a more modern spelling in which the letter "h" has been added to indicate the special pronunciation of the "m" as a "w" or "v" sound. The pronunciation of both remains [saw-en].

Vowels
á = ah of "father"
a = as above but shorter
é as in "they"
e as in "get"
í as "ee" in "greet"
i as in "hit"
ó as in "go"
o as in "hot"
ú as "oo" in "food"
u as in "full"
ai = a in first syllable, and as "y" in "fly" elsewhere
iu = u with i only slightly sounded
ui = i but with the u slightly sounded
ei = e

Diphthongs
ae, ai, oe, oi = aw + ee, similar to the sound of -oy in "boy" and the -igh in "high".

The Book of Ogham

Consonants
Here are the pronunciation of the consonants according to their position in words – whether the first letter, in the middle of a word, or in final position.

Letter	Initial	Medial	Final
c	as k	as g	as g
p	as p	as b	as b
b	as b	as v or w	as v or w
d	as d	as th in "this"	as th in "this"
t	as t	as d	as d
g	hard as in "get"	as a gargled gh	as medial
m	m (very nasal)	as mv (nasal)	as medial

Consonants are slender where an e or i precedes or follows. Consonants which are aspirated are sometimes spelled with either a dot above them or with an h immediately after them.

Aspirated Consonants
ch = the guttural ch of "loch"; when slender as the ch in German "ich"
ph = as f in "fun"; "fy" sound as in "feud" when slender
th = th in "think" (silent in more modern Irish)
fh = this is silent, but sometimes it is a faint breathing
sh = as the h in "hit"; when slender, it sound like the h in "hue"

Unaspirated Consonants
f = as in English, as "fy" sound in "feud" when slender
s = as in "sing", never as in "roses"; but when followed by or preceding an e or i, as the "sh" in "shoe"
r = trilled r as in Scottish pronunciation
ng = as in "singer", not as in "finger"
mb = mm; this sound is also sometimes spelled mm
nd = nn; this sound is also sometimes spelled nn
l = as in "lay"
h = is often silent, or pronounced as a faint breathing sound

212

The Book of Ogham

Examples of most of the variants in Old Irish pronunciation are given in the phonetic transcriptions of the words given in the glossary.

The Book of Ogham

The Book of Ogham

Bibliography

Calder, G. Auraicept na N'Eces. Edinburgh: John Grant, 1917.

Caesar, Julius. The Conquest of Gaul. Harmondsworth, UK: Penguin, 1951.

Chadwick, Nora. The Celts. Harmondsworth, UK: Penguin, 1970.

Cross, Tom P. and Slover, Clark H. eds. Ancient Irish Tales. Dublin: Figgis, 1936. (AIT)

Davidson, H.R.E. Myths and Symbols in Pagan Europe. Syracuse: University of Syracuse Press, 1988.

Delaney, Frank. The Celts. Boston: Little Brown, 1986.

Derolez, René. Runica Manuscripta. Brugge: Rijksuniversiteit te Gent, 1954.

De Vries, Jan. Keltische Religion. Stuttgart: Kohlhammer, 1961.

Eliade, Mircea. Shamanism: Archaic Techniques of Ecstasy. Harmondsworth, UK: Penguin, 1964.

Eluäre, Christiane. The Celts: First Master of Europe. New York: Thames and Hudson, 1993.

Falconar, A.E.I. Celtic Tales of Myth and Fantasy. Isle of Man: Non-Aristotelean Publishing, 1984.

Flowers, Stephen E. Celtic Revivals: From Dawn to Twilight. Smithville: Runa-Raven. [Forthcoming 2006.]

Gantz, Jeffrey, trans. The Mabinogion. Harmondsworth, UK: Penguin, 1976.

Geoffrey of Monmouth. Histories of the Kings of Britain. London: J.M. Dent & Sons, 1911.

Goodenough, Simon. Celtic Mythology. Twickenham, UK: Tiger Books International, 1997.

Graves, Robert. The White Goddess. New York: Farrar, Strauss and Girous, 1966. 2nd ed. [orig. published 1948.]

Green, Miranda. The Gods of the Celts. Stroud, UK: Sutton Publishing, 1986.

Grieve, M.A. A Modern Herbal. New York: Dover, 1971. [orig. published 1931.]

Hall Caine, W. Ralph. Annals of the Magic Isle. London: Cecil

The Book of Ogham

Palmer, 1926.

Lehmann, Ruth P. and Winfrid P. Lehmann. An Introduction to Old Irish. New York: The Modern Language Association, 1975.

Littleton, C.S. The New Comparative Mythology. Berkeley: University of California Press, 1982.

Lysaght, Patricia. A Pocket Book of the Banshee. Dublin: O'Brien, 1998.

Macalister, R.A. Stewart. The Secret Languages of Ireland. Cambridge: Cambridge University Press, 1937.

Macalister, R.A. Stewart. Corpus inscriptionem insularum celticarum. Dublin: Irish Manuscripts Commission, 1945.

Maccrossan, Tadhg. The Sacred Cauldron: Secrets of the Druids. St. Paul, MN: Llewellyn, 1991.

McManus, Damien. Guide to Ogam. Maynooth: An Sagart, 1991.

McManus, Damien. "Irish Letter-Names and Their Kennings." Ériu 37 (1988), pp. 127-168.

Matthews, Caitlin. The Elements of the Celtic Tradition. Longmead, UK: Element Books, 1989.

Matthews, John and Caitlin. The Aquarian Guide to British and Irish Mythology. Wellingborough, UK: Aquarian, 1988.

Murray, Liz and Colin. The Celtic Tree Oracle. London: Rider, 1988.

Pennick, Nigel. Games of the Gods: The Origins of Board Games in Magic and Divination. York Beach, ME: Weiser, 1989.

Piggott, Stuart. The Druids. London: Thames and Hudson, 1968.

Rees, Alwyn and Brinley. Celtic Heritage: Ancient Tradition in Ireland and Wales. London: Thames and Hudson, 1961.

Thorsson, Edred. Runelore: A Handbook of Esoteric Runology. York Beach, ME: Weiser, 1987.

Tolstoy, Nikolai. The Quest For Merlin. Boston: Little Brown, 1985.

The Book of Ogham

The Book of Ogham

Printed in Great Britain
by Amazon.co.uk, Ltd.,
Marston Gate.